DON'T LET THE MONSTERS OUT

AN AMERICAN AIRMAN'S DESCENT INTO DARKNESS AT CAMP BUCCA, IRAQ

HEATHER O'BRIEN

D1738100

CONTENTS

To Annette, Alex, and Sandy: More than once, you helped me fight off my monsters even while fighting your own. This is as much your story as it is mine.

Freedom!

And to Michael and John: Thank you.

ACKNOWLEDGMENTS

God: He alone could redeem my story into something that will hopefully help others. Because of Him, this isn't the end of my story but only the beginning.

My parents: You were the first readers of this crazy manuscript and the first to encourage me to publish. I cannot imagine what it must be like to read this and realize your baby girl is the person in the story. Thanks for encouraging me that this is a story worth telling.

Lisa Thompson: It takes a certain faith to agree to read a manuscript based solely on a phone call and a voicemail. The amount of time, energy, effort, and creativity you have put into this writing has made it immeasurably better. All your advice and nuggets of wisdom have found a home in my writing style from now on. Thank you.

Annette Hannah: My sister from another mister. To hell and back again, we've had each other's backs. You even so generously agreed to rip open the Band-aid of Bucca and read this book.

Rachel Newhouse: You read a manuscript from some crazy daughter of a friend and saw that it was worth salvaging. Your conversations and step-by-step breakdown of this whole wild process have been invaluable.

Dean'na Wantz: You've been a wonderful sounding board and source of encouragement. From reading all the ick that is this book to your hugs that heal the soul, you have been a source of godly strength and comfort.

INTRODUCTION

Even after fifteen years, I can still smell it. On good days, it takes me a while, but it's still there: the undeniable scent of sweat, filth, burning trash, and hatred. Yes, hatred. Hatred has a smell, a smell like rotten oranges covered in flammable oil or like hot tea poured into a plate of dirt and formed into granite balls. But more often than not, on the bad days or even regular days, I wake up to the faint smell vanishing with my dreams. The smell of Camp Bucca.

Camp Bucca is the base no one wants to talk about. Books have been written by many soldiers, marines, reporters, and a myriad of others about the war in Iraq. IEDs, mortar attacks, and house-to-house combat have all been discussed hundreds of times over. These books have done a great job of educating the public who never served. I have even read and own many. But it's a scarcity to find a book about this deployment. No one wants to think about what happens when the enemy is not killed but captured. Everyone knows the scandal of Abu Graib, but what about Camp Bucca? Most of the public has never even heard of that base, because there was no huge scandal. Unlike Abu Graib, this base had no torture allegations, yet Camp Bucca at its peak housed over two and one-half times more detainees than Abu Graib.

Some people say they know about Camp Bucca. It rapidly became known as the birthplace of ISIS. And it's true, the major infrastructure and backbone of ISIS were created in Camp Bucca. Almost all the major players were imprisoned there at some point. These extremists easily formed a new resistance; Iraqis were detained at an alarming rate. If they were even suspected of participating in a crime, they could be arrested and left in these internment facilities for years. As the largest facility, Camp Bucca held the most disillusioned inmates. Charismatic leaders like Al-Baghdadi could easily radicalize them. He was merely a flame to dry wood. The airmen, soldiers, and seamen stationed there worked as hard as they could to stop groups from forming, but it was not enough. They didn't have enough people or resources to stop it. Detainees came by the thousands. At the height of the Surge in 2007, we were getting more than three thousand inmates monthly; it was simply impossible to stem the flow. We were frightfully understaffed and required to let the detainees deal with each other and leave us alone as much as possible. This hands-off approach was a breeding ground for ISIS.

This isn't a deployment story about convoys, IEDS, or rockets (well, not many). Instead, it's the deployment story of thousands of

Army MPs, Air Force Security Forces, and Navy Seamen and how they fought ISIS at its birthplace. This is the story of how good people slowly turned into monsters to keep other monsters at bay. War might be hell, but detainee operations are a Greek tragedy where no one escapes unscathed and even the hero can become the villain.

CHAPTER ONE

ORIGINS

"The second World Trade Tower has just collapsed." My government teacher, Mr. Young, had just stopped class. Moments earlier, another teacher had interrupted his lesson. After a hurried, whispered conversation, he told us to grab our stuff and follow them to the art classroom where there was a TV. We looked at each other, shrugging our shoulders at his pale and shaken expression, but no one dared ask what was happening.

That was my first image on September 11, 2001, a quick video as police and firefighters walked into a building and its sudden collapse on them. Some people watched in stunned silence. Others watched with jaws dropped or tears streaming down their cheeks. Still others muttered under their breath, their cheeks red. My world was going to change; America was going to war.

I grew up in an Army town; St. Robert, Missouri, sits right next to Fort Leonard Wood. Most of the men and women I knew had served or were serving in the Army. My father was no exception; he had been active duty for a while and was in the reserves. Military service was typical in my town; in fact, many high school graduates had already completed basic training by the time they finished high school. St. Robert is a small town with few prospects for a high school graduate; not everyone could get scholarships for college. If you weren't smart or athletic, then you either worked at Wal-Mart or joined the military.

At the beginning of my senior year, I had checked with a couple of recruiters but was noncommittal about joining the military. Then September 11 happened. Suddenly, the idea of joining the military wasn't so terrible; in fact, it sounded pretty damn great. I decided to go into the Air Force; I couldn't even sit on a Ferris wheel without blacking out, but at least, I wouldn't walk as much as they did in the Army. Choosing a job was easy; I had always wanted to be in law enforcement, so I signed up for Security Forces. I could be a cop and follow in two of my grandfathers' footsteps. Underscoring that drive was a desire to see justice served for people like my friend, Janet, who was murdered along with her baby early in our senior year. In December 2001, when I signed up, women couldn't be in combat roles, so Security Forces was one of the closest jobs to combat for a woman.

I waited until after graduation to jump into basic training in May 2002. Ten days later, I was on a plane bound for San Antonio, Texas. Basic training and technical school were both at the same place, Lackland Air Force Base right outside San Antonio. I was in Texas from May to September. All our training, including terror drills and double- and triple-checking identification, emphasized that we were a nation at war.

My first assignment was to Kadena AFB in Okinawa, Japan. The instructor's constant reminder that we would most assuredly see combat immediately after graduation almost made this assignment to the Pacific theater a bit of a letdown. I was lucky enough to travel with two guys from my tech school, so I initially had some people to hang out with. During the next two years, I walked around a lot of planes and stood at gates, checking IDs. This wasn't quite the awesome cop job I thought I signed up for. I couldn't really complain though; I lived on a tropical island where a beach was never more than two miles away. We had weekly beach bonfires, keg parties, and surfing trips.

About ten months into my time at Kadena, in fall 2003, I was told to prepare for my first deployment. The US had invaded Iraq, and every branch of service was tasked with combat operations. Initially, our deployment was to Tikrit, Iraq. My heart pounded; finally, I could go fight terrorists.

Suddenly, our orders changed; now we were headed to a small base in Pakistan. I didn't even realize we had US forces in Pakistan; in fact, no one at my base had ever even heard of Shahbaz AFB outside Jacobabad. Later, I found out that no one had heard of this base because our government patently denied ever having a base in Pakistan. Operation Iraqi Freedom would have to wait; I was headed to Operation Enduring Freedom.

J-Bad—what we called Shahbaz—was tiny, less than a mile long and a mile wide. We had slightly over 250 personnel on the entire base with no actual stationed aircraft. This meant that if the town of more than three hundred thousand people wanted to attack us, our closest air support was four hours away. In essence, we were fucked. Possible brutal imminent death aside, J-Bad was like summer camp with high school pranks and guns. I was bitten by the deployment bug and wanted nothing more than to deploy again and again. It was a perfect first combat tour, complete with living in tents and shitty food. There, I first learned that no matter your original orders, Air Force deployments for cops were inevitably extended, which for me was from four months to almost eight months.

In November 2004, my assignment to Kadena ended, and I was relocated to Minot, North Dakota. When I stepped off the plane with only a light jacket, the ground outside was completely blanketed in snow; in fact, I never saw the ground until the next April. Overnight,

I went from 86 degrees to -15 degrees; Uncle Sam has a sick sense of humor. The fastest way out of Minot was by re-enlisting and getting what's called Base of Preference (BOP). This was simply a contract with the Air Force, stating that on my re-enlistment, I would get orders to one of eight requested bases. I got lucky number eight, Little Rock AFB (LRAFB), Arkansas.

Little Rock was only a five-hour drive from my hometown, and Security Forces there deployed regularly, which was exactly what I wanted. I reported to LRAFB in February 2006 as an E-4 or Senior Airman and was eligible to promote to Staff Sergeant if I passed the promotion tests. I had been in the Air Force a little less than four years and had already been on one deployment and to three different bases. I had done everything, including flightline security, base defense, nuclear missile security, and law enforcement; I thought I knew everything about my career field. The younger airmen on my flight had taken to calling me Grandma because I had been to so many different bases in such a short time. Plus, the budding arthritis in my joints probably helped the name stick.

In August 2006, I passed the Air Force Promotion Test and was slated to promote to Staff Sergeant in May 2007. In October, I was told I would be deploying by early January to a base called Camp Bucca, Iraq. I would be twenty-three years old and in charge of airman in one of the most dangerous places on earth. I was about to find out how little I really knew about my job and especially about myself.

CHAPTER TWO

PLANES, NO TRAINS, AND UPSIDE-DOWN HUMVEES

O ur deployment training took place in two locations: Camp McGregor, New Mexico, and Fort Lewis, Washington. Pre-deployment training is incredibly important, not only for preparing for unique situations your team might find themselves in but also because the Air Force Security Forces don't deploy by squadrons. In the Army, Marines, and even the Navy, units usually deploy together. Not so in the Air Force, especially as Security Forces. We deploy generally as squads: three fire teams consisting of four people in each team and one squad leader. Bases may send two or three squads but rarely more than that. Security Forces deployed often, but we only had police and Security Forces at our base. If our commander sent too many cops, there would not be enough left to cover the base.

While pre-deployment training is necessary for all the squads to begin the blending process, for a deployment like ours, it was critical. Except only half of our team was together. The larger half, our whole leadership team, was down in New Mexico where I was while the rest of the team was training up in Ft. Lewis. We had been pulled from bases all over the world: my team members were from Little Rock,

Arkansas, and others were from Hill, Utah; Kadena, Okinawa; Andrews, Washington, DC; Yokota, Japan; Hickam, Hawaii; and Holloman, New Mexico. Ironically, one of the two squads from Holloman was sent to Ft. Lewis. One squad literally drove three-and-a-half hours to McGregor while the other squad had to fly a thousand miles north. It made no sense whatsoever. But that was the Air Force way.

Our training began around the beginning of January 2007, and lasted for about three-and-a-half weeks. Camp McGregor is in the middle of Nowhere, New Mexico; the base had only a small little Shoppette and a gym. There was nothing to do, which was fine because we didn't have much downtime. We trained every day with only a half day on Sundays.

Camp McGregor was a necessary wake-up call. We had to march everywhere, which Air Force people normally didn't do. We also had to wear our gear, helmet, flak vest, gas mask, and weapons everywhere we went. It was tiring, but I'm very glad we did; we got used to wearing our equipment for hours in Iraq. Everyone knew that Camp Bucca was an internment facility but not much more. Some people knew others who had been there before, but those people wouldn't tell us too much. I knew a few guys from Little Rock who had been to Bucca; in fact, Little Rock routinely sent squads to Bucca. The guys who had been there weren't very talkative about it either.

One airman that I had been working with one shift would only say, "Everyone wants to kill you." The sergeant in charge of making sure we had all our gear before deploying had been to Bucca and kept reminding us to watch our backs. Even before we got to training, we were reminded to be careful. This was the second deployment to Bucca for one of our teammates; his normal joking, easy-going demeanor was replaced by a seriousness I had never seen in him. He absorbed everything the trainers talked about as if it were the most important information he had ever heard. My stomach began to do nervous twisty flips the longer no one would tell us anything; my deployment diet started early on. How was I supposed to lead and keep airmen safe in an environment that no one would even talk about?

I was lucky that I was deploying with someone who would become one of my closest friends, Staff Sergeant Taylor Ray. We were both from Little Rock, but due to working completely opposite schedules had never really hung out before deploying. We are basically polar opposites in appearance: She is fair-haired, taller, and thinner but very wiry; I am dark-haired, short, and stocky. She could run for days, and I could ruck march forever. Even our attitudes were different: She thinks through her actions; I am rash and reckless. But somehow, we became fast friends almost instantly. If you were looking for me, find Taylor or vice versa because we were always around each other. We both love the movie *First Wives' Club* and throughout our deployment, we would throw out lines to see how far we could keep the dialogue going. We almost memorized the whole damn movie.

We were housed in barracks at McGregor, which held all the females from every base. Taylor's squad arrived before mine, and due to her quick actions, she scored a six-man room for most of the females on our two squads. Most of the other rooms were four-man rooms. The upside to our bigger room was we had a shower and toilet while all the other rooms had to share the group facilities. The bathroom was a hidden gem; not only did we have private showers, but the chow hall made powdered eggs every morning, which gave everyone indigestion. A little privacy when your body is losing everything it ever consumed is precious. We just had to make sure to stagger our eating times so we all didn't need the bathroom at once. And no one ever showered in the morning; steam with that concoction would have been lethal.

This was only my second deployment, but it was the first one where I saw more than one female senior non-commissioned officer (SNCO). At McGregor, we had at least three Technical Sergeants or Techs (TSgt) for short. That might not seem that impressive, but I had been in for three years before I saw a female SNCO. At my first duty station, there was only one female NCO on a flight of about forty-five people on our shift.

In addition to our long workdays, we were responsible for cleaning the barracks every day. The Tech Sergeants broke it down fairly by rotating bases every day. So each squad only had cleaning duty three times during training. The first night, our squad did clean up. I had volunteered to mop, which I liked because it was the last thing to do, so I got to laze around while the rest of the squad was cleaning. I was standing in the hallway with my mop and bucket, chatting and laughing with Taylor and some others when one of the Techs materialized next to me. One minute, there was nobody, and the next, TSgt Holmes was standing right next to me.

That's how TSgt Holmes is though: silent and almost invisible until she wants you to see her. She is dark-haired like me and tall and has incredibly intense hazel eyes. She had a "don't fuck with me" attitude that made her quite intimidating. "Airman O'Brien, why aren't you doing any clean up?" she calmly asked me.

Laughing, I turned to her. "Don't worry, Sarge, I'm going to mop in a few. I've got this." All my life, I have had problems with my mouth getting me into trouble, whether it was on the playground, insulting bigger kids or stupidly telling the NCO to let me take care of this. NCOs have the power to make life hell; they can even make others' lives hell because of you. This ensures that your life is continued hell because the others will get you after the NCO leaves. Telling a person two ranks above me not to worry was akin to saying, "Fuck you, I know better than you." It was a challenge of a sort, and no NCO can let a challenge go unanswered.

She became deadly quiet. "Do you want me to break the handle, stick it in your ass, and mop the floor with your head, or will you start mopping now?" I started mopping immediately! To this day, I'm not sure if she was joking, but it was the beginning of a beautiful friendship. That doesn't sound like a way to become friends, but the threats and language were just par for the course in the military. TSgt Holmes kept getting assigned to groups that Taylor and I were in, and she slowly relaxed a bit around us. Most women in the military don't really get into the catty games that a lot of nonmilitary women do. Many times, we are simply excited to have other women around in a world of men.

Every morning, we were bused for miles to training trailers in the middle of nowhere. Scruffy small trees and foothills surrounded the area. Since it was the middle of winter, we would freeze while waiting for the training trailers to be unlocked. The insides weren't much warmer, so we got used to wearing all our cold weather gear along with our daily gear. Well, almost everyone wore their cold-weather sweaters and thermals but not Little Rock people. Due to an ordering error somewhere, we only had our jackets but no thermals, gloves, hats, or sweaters. We finally got our stuff, though, two days before we left for Kuwait. During the breaks, we gathered around the smoking area and packed in for heat. Those 20-degree days in the open land of Camp McGregor ensured that almost everyone became a smoker.

One portion of our training was a seventy-two-hour exercise where we would run a mock prison filled with Iraqis, contractors paid to act like terrorists. These actors were mostly Hispanic and were all fluent in Spanish. They only spoke Spanish around us to simulate being around people who didn't understand English. Unfortunately, this was not exactly the same since almost everyone knew at least a little Spanish. We thought that communication wouldn't be that hard with Arabic speakers. How terribly wrong we were.

I was part of the night shift, and our watch was from 1800 hours to 0600 hours. One night, it snowed—actual snow with accumulation in southern New Mexico, a weather event that only happened once every twenty-five years. And we still didn't have our cold-weather gear; I was already a little sick, but those freezing, snowy nights made it much worse. One upside was that during a fake mortar attack on the snowy night, I was "injured" and sent to the inside of a training trailer for three hours. The instructors in there had the heat cranked up and gave us hot cocoa and coffee. When my three hours were up, I tried to bargain with the instructor, saying I thought my injury had taken a turn for the worse. No luck. I was sent back, but at least my clothes had dried, and it was almost dawn.

Some days, the weather gave us the best of both worlds: freezing in the morning and 55 to 60 by noon. The constantly fluctuating temperatures made a lot of us sick and me worse. We could only go to the medical station before or after training because if you missed training, you might not deploy. I tried my damndest not to go to the med station, but finally my roommates had enough of my hacking and wheezing, so they forced me to go. All they gave me were some Hall's throat drops, Motrin, and instructions to rest. I laughed at the directions to rest as our training days lasted from fourteen to sixteen hours.

However it was New Mexico after all, so for about a week, we had beautiful weather: sunny, no clouds, and in the 60s. Unfortunately, this was when my group was scheduled to do our pepper spray training. The sunnier it was, the worse the pepper spray felt. On the day of our OC evaluation, there wasn't a cloud in the sky. We had to line up in a single-file line and watch as each person got sprayed. After being sprayed, the person then had to successfully navigate through a course of takedowns and defense from the instructors in order to pass and move on. I wanted to be the first one to do it, not as a show-off but because the morning's powdered eggs were threatening to reappear the more I watched other people react to getting sprayed.

But the higher-ranking personnel went first so they could show us how it was done. It was scary watching these grown men, big guys all muscled up, completely incapacitated by this spray. But the women seemed to be able to take the shock of pepper spray a little better than some of the guys. I asked a friend of mine why that was, and she said, "I think it's because guys aren't used to being physically powerless. We females have learned how to use our minds more than our physicality." That made sense to me, but all I could think about was that this would not feel good.

I was next—the eggs had moved from my belly into my throat and were playing a game called "What Do I Taste Like Now?" as I prepared to be hit. As a last reminder, the instructor said, "No swearing allowed, Senior Airman. One or two slips are acceptable, but after that, you have to redo the course."

Damn! I thought. I was so nervous about the OC that I forgot about the swearing rule. *Psht!* Grimy, rough orange OC smacked into my eyebrows.

"Eyes open!" Breathing in, I popped open my eyes. No pain. So far, so good. I advanced to the first person to take down and handily subdued him.

All right, I can do this. No problem! I started heading to the next guy.

"Stop there! Now look at me and close your eyes," the sergeant said. Closed, easy did it. "Now open them." As I opened them, suddenly, pain shot through them and into my skull. It felt as if burning sandpaper were grinding my eyes into blindness.

"Oh fuck," I yelled, "fuck, fuck, fuck!"

"Easy, Airman, remember you will have to go back to the beginning if you keep swearing."

"Fuck. Sorry, but damn! Sorry, I don't have any other words." The sergeant laughed but tried to be quiet, which only enraged me more. A fire consumed me that had nothing to do with my burning eyes. I allowed the fire to burn away the pukey egg taste and fill me with a white-hot steel will that drove me to finish the rest of the course, and thankfully, I didn't have to redo it. I had just learned my first important lesson; anger will get the job done when you feel too weak.

Later that night, I was recounting the day for Taylor, my battle buddy. This was a military term used to designate your closest friend or the person who would always know where you were. Battle buddies were simply pairs or small groups that were always together; it was a way of ensuring everyone's safety. She was laughing and having a great time at my expense when I reminded her, she had the OC spray lane in just a couple of more days. I kept joking that I would take her picture when she got back from the course. I upheld my promise.

Later that evening, we were back in the barracks for the night, and I was getting ready to shower. As soon as I stepped in the shower, I realized my mistake. The instructors had told us to make sure we washed off our faces and necks very thoroughly before showering. If we missed any of the OC spray, it might react to more hot water and spread. Sure enough, that's what happened. I felt as if I had fire ants all over my body. All I could do was continue to wash and try to get it all off while trying to stop it from spreading to any more sensitive areas. By the yelps and hollers coming from other showers, I wasn't the only one in the same predicament.

One great side effect of the pepper spray, though, was that it momentarily cleared out my severe sinus infection and cough. For about three days, I could breathe again. My roommates loved the fact that my snoring temporarily stopped. Food tasted amazing—even the evil powdered eggs and our nasty MREs had a yummy flavor. I could even smell body funk and sweat again; that I hadn't really missed. But after a few days, my symptoms crept right back, and I was back to a hacking cough.

As training progressed, we began to get reports from Camp Bucca.

Our commander was in touch with the current commander there, and he read about any new situations and briefed us on what we might need to expect. The first few reports weren't bad: The detainees were a little restless, one or two attempted to escape, blah, blah, blah. Then the reports changed. First there was a riot, then two. Next, detainees were actively trying to attack the guards. Then, our entire squadron was called into a mandatory Commander's Call right at the end of the duty day. Our commander briefed us that within the last forty-eight hours, two Navy personnel had committed suicide. This was the first briefing where he told us, if we weren't mentally ready for what was about to happen, then we needed to tell our leadership to send us home. But he knew going home was not an option. And there was no way to know if we were mentally ready until the shit hit the fan.

He then released all the airmen and told all the NCOs to stay. I got ready to leave since I wasn't promoting to Staff Sergeant until May, so technically, I was still an airman. The commander paused. "If you're promoting within this deployment, you stay too."

Dammit! I slunk back to my seat. For the next hour, he stressed the importance of making sure we looked after our airmen. Once we got to Bucca, we wouldn't necessarily be with people from our home bases. We were instructed to make sure we knew all our airmen's home units and where to find their emergency contact info. But mainly, he stressed making sure we checked up on them. "Make sure they know they can come to you with an issue. Make sure you know them well enough to know when something is not right."

Right after these reports and this briefing, I realized this would not be a normal deployment. The emphasis that our leadership and Army trainers placed on keeping ourselves and our people safe began to sink in. Our instructors constantly emphasized remaining professional at all times, and when we couldn't anymore, tell our leaders. Not *if* we couldn't but *when*—they obviously knew something we didn't know yet. The prison may not hurt you physically, but if you let it, it would break you mentally. I resolved not to let that happen; I wouldn't be the broken airman with a sad story for every day of the week. Those detainees wouldn't break me—nothing would.

I wondered how crappy Camp Bucca was that not one but two people killed themselves only a few weeks before going home. Was it really all that bad? Or was our Commander just trying to keep us on our toes? What had I gotten myself into?

While I couldn't find out a lot about Camp Bucca and the prison, I did know that we had lost two airmen there. In 2006, Airman First Class (A1C) Carl Ware had been killed when another airman recklessly discharged his firearm. Because of his negligence, that airman was sentenced to ten years in prison. In 2005, A1C Elizabeth Jacobson was killed by an IED during a convoy outside Bucca. She was assigned to the same squadron we would be going to; she had volunteered to do additional duty on convoys. She was the first female Security Forces Airman to die in combat since the Vietnam War.

The closer we got to our leave date, the more I thought of the two factors that proved so lethal: enemy action and complacency. I couldn't control insurgents and detainees, but I could control my vigilance; no one would be knocking on my parents' door because I got lazy. I had no idea how much that decision would be tested in the following months.

We flew out of Ft. Bliss, Texas, and stopped in Bangor, Maine, to switch planes. As we walked off the plane, we were greeted by dozens of people. They broke into cheers and clapping as soon as they saw us. Someone explained they were volunteers from the community who were there to greet every plane deploying and coming home. Many of them were veterans of Vietnam and Korea, some were spouses of veterans, and some were just citizens. This community had made a pact to ensure that no service member ever arrived or left their airport without being greeted and thanked. They had been doing this ever since 2003; a military plane has never landed there without someone to greet it, no matter the time of day or night.

These amazing people did more than just greet us, though; they gave us homemade snacks, treats, and pillows for the plane. If someone needed to make a phone call home, they gave us phones to use. They also handed out phone cards for when we got to Kuwait and Iraq. But perhaps the best thing of all was they simply were there. They talked with us, cried, hugged a few, and looked at people's photos of their families. They genuinely cared. As we readied to board our next plane, no one got on that ramp without a warm hug and a "come home soon and safe" speech. Then we walked up the ramp, and they started clapping and cheering again. I snuck a look back and more than a few of them were wiping their eyes. It was like we had walked into every WW2 movie with a going-away or a homecoming scene. We were American heroes going off to fight the big bad evil; when I close my eyes, I can still see their faces and hear their goodbyes. I can talk to others on the deployment, and they remember the same thing. I didn't know it then, but this would be one of the last times I felt America cared for us.

After a quick stop in Germany, we landed in Kuwait City International Airport (KCIA) sometime after dark. After traveling through so many time zones, I had no idea what time it was, but I knew it was February 2007. Time was already a useless measurement. I had just arrived, and yet it seemed I had always been in Kuwait. We got off the plane and stayed on the flightline until buses arrived to pick us up. We were not allowed into the airport as a safety precaution; spies were everywhere, trying to figure out American troop movements. Plus, we would be sitting ducks for an extremist group. Unlike Pakistan, we flew into Kuwait with our weapons all neatly packed away and completely useless.

After about sixteen hours of flying, I was happy to finally be able to fully stand up and walk around, but I should have used the bathroom before exiting the plane. No big deal though, I would just go once we got to Camp Buehring. However, I didn't realize that the trip would take almost two hours! Once the buses arrived, we piled into them and started our long drive. These were luxury buses with really tall hoods and nice comfortable seats. They even had a bathroom, which was a relief because I wasn't the only one who needed to use it. But there were a couple of problems: The toilet was only a box with a hole on top to squat over, and there were no lights. One poor sucker was so bad off that she attempted to use the facilities but ended up almost falling off the bucket and pissed all over the little room. My initial flightline training from Kadena came screaming back to me. The one female NCO yelled at all the females on shift: "We have to prove that we can hang tough with the guys. There is no room for whiners! Pee when you can, hold it when you can't, and no fucking whining!" I heard that speech more times than I can count. The words varied, but the meaning behind them was the same: Keep up with the men or get out. We all had to suffer until we got to the air base; it wouldn't have been so bad except the driver kept bouncing the bus all over the damn road.

As soon as we entered the base, we demanded that our bus driver find the nearest toilets. He pulled over, and we jumped off, running into what we would later find out was the officer's bathroom area. We didn't even care if it was a guys' or girls' bathroom; they all had stalls, so we just went into whichever one had the shortest line. I released the ocean that had built up inside me; seriously, I even cried a little. Afterward, we were bused to the transient living area, big tents, which we would be staying in until we headed into Iraq.

The rest of our team that trained in Ft. Lewis met us there about twenty-four hours later. Finally, we were all united, in total, more than four hundred Security Forces. Since our career field wasn't the largest grouping, many of us had friends from other deployments, old duty stations, former supervisors, etc. It was like a little crazed-cop reunion. I ran into two people from my first base. Shawn and I had deployed from Kadena to Pakistan, where we hung out a lot. Amanda Lowell was another good friend who actually looked so much like me that we were often dubbed "the twins" at Kadena. We spent time catching up.

We were stuck at the wonderful Camp Buehring, Kuwait, while awaiting our transfer to Camp Bucca. Really, this base had actual restaurants; Green Beans Coffee, which I actually liked better than Starbucks; and some shops. Our living arrangements were like any other transit group; we lived in these gargantuan tents that easily fit up to fifty people. All the women had enough room to store our cots, gear, and weapons in one tent. Lying down, I could extend my arms and touch the person on either side of me—quite roomy compared to the men's tents. We would only be there a few days. The guys were crammed like sardines into four tents at about seventy to a group. I opened the door to one; it looked like overcrowding at a concert with DCUs, duffel bags, and weapons. It was one of the few times I was thankful to be a woman in a male-dominated career.

The tents were acceptable, but the bathrooms were not. Since we were in the transit area, we did not get the shower–latrine cadillac. Cadillacs are a type of permanent yet mobile trailer divided in half with showers and toilets, a constantly steamy cesspool of running water and someone with the shits. We had an old version—with mold everywhere—that was only showers. Trench foot became a real threat. But despite the gross conditions, we could live with it for a few days. We had Porta Johns for toilets; they were not new or even clean but were what nightmares are made of. I'm not snooty—I've used Porta Johns and outhouses and even made my own little spot when needed. I wouldn't have minded if they were a little stinky or funky. But these had old feces on the seats and near the toilet paper roll. Guys just peed on the ledge in there.

Later, I found out that the Kuwaiti base workers would sneak over to these instead of using the ones in their work area. One night, when I went to use the bathroom in desperation due to increased water consumption, I knocked and heard nothing, so I opened the door. Like a deer in headlights, a Kuwaiti was squatting on top of the ledge. I managed to say, "Whoops!" and walked away. I found another one that was thankfully empty and did my business. After that, I never went to those Porta Johns unless I had a battle buddy with me.

While at Camp Buehring, we had to complete a few more trainings, mostly PowerPoint lectures. We also went through Humvee rollover training, a nice two-hour lecture that included grotesque images of deadly accidents. The trainers made sure to show that video right before lunch. The last portion of the day, we actually conducted an actual rollover done in a specialized Humvee attached to a large turning bar. Five of us got in the Humvee. Once the vehicle began flipping, we screamed, "Rollover, rollover, rollover!" We then each grabbed an extremity of the gunner, pulled them in, and held them safely until the vehicle slowed to a stop—upside down. Afterward, each member attempted to find a way out and assist the others out.

More than a few of us cracked heads and faces on unforgiving metal when we forgot to brace ourselves before unbuckling the seat belts. I spent what felt like an eternity (but was only a minute or so), kicking at the windshield instead of at my driver's door. Even in those few seconds, claustrophobia grabbed ahold of me. Everything was upside down and backwards; my brain couldn't process what had happened. It became very clear how people could drown in a rollover. But altogether, it was one of the more fun training activities.

In another training exercise, we went off base to sight in our M4s. We shot maybe ten to fifteen rounds, just enough to check that our weapons were still working correctly. Occasionally, when firing, our range instructors (some of our higher-ranking NCOs) had to stop the firing due to camels wandering onto the range. Apparently, when the military set up the range, they accidentally put it right in the middle of a nomadic tribe's camel route. After about ten minutes of firing in slow bursts and checking for any issues, we were cleared. We still had a few rounds of ammo left, so our range instructors passed those out, and we fired as needed. Right then, a herd of camels came sauntering through the range just behind the targets. Our range instructors yelled at us to stop, and almost everyone did. Only one person—the supposedly not-sick bronchial-coughing, ear-plugged Senior Airman —didn't hear the call. I accidentally killed a camel, murdered the poor sucker right on his way to the watering hole.

Our range instructor, TSgt Holmes, came down and smacked my head, which was the signal to cease fire. She yelled, "Did you not hear me calling the cease fire?"

"No, TSgt Holmes, I really can't hear anything."

"You killed a camel!"

"What?"

"You just slaughtered a damn camel!" We had to wait almost an hour on the buses before leaving while TSgt Holmes dealt with some angry tribal leaders. We weren't even in Iraq yet, and I had my first kill. Ironically, on our ride back to the camp, we kept seeing dead camels on the side of the road. I guess if cars hit them all the time, one accidental shooting wasn't too bad. This was yet another way that locals got one over the US government. One dead camel equaled a lot of money for a nomad.

At one of our last squadron briefings, we were assigned to our new compounds and told to get together with our new groups. Leadership had posted each compound roster and taped it up in the front of the tent. I went around to almost every paper but couldn't find my name. Throat dry, I asked one of the Master Sergeants at the front if he had any clue what compound I was in. He got my name, told me to wait, and went and got another Master Sergeant who was already addressing his group. As they walked toward me, they were discussing whether I was the right O'Brien. The new Master Sergeant asked how many other O'Briens were in the squadron. I told him, "None, just me. Sarge, you're in charge of the QRF team, right?" Then I looked at him.

He said, "Yep, and I guess you're in it now too."

I laughed. "When you saw SrA O'Brien, you thought it was a guy, huh?" He kind of chuckled and said he did. "Don't worry, Sarge, you aren't the first or last who thought that!" At my first duty station, the guy assigned to pick me up at the airport walked by me three times because he thought O'Brien was a guy. This has happened to me more times than I can count.

Almost every detainee was assigned to a compound, according to their ethnicity or religious faction. Leadership tried to keep each particular group isolated from the others in order to stop them from banding together. But QRF (Quick Response Force) was different. If an incident occurred in any part of the TIF (Theater Internment Facility), we were the rapid-response team. We also conducted a host of other jobs, such as in- and out-processing detainees, compound searches, compound digs (tunnel hunting), and any other tasks that the compounds needed help with. I thought riot control would be the craziest job. I couldn't wait. I could not become complacent, and I wanted that action so I could stay focused at all times. The only downside was that Taylor was going to Compound 10, and TSgt Holmes was headed to Compound 8, so I wouldn't be seeing them too often. A large group of Security Forces had been at Bucca almost four months, and they would be staying with us for most of our deployment. Many of them were in QRF, so many of us didn't know each other.

A couple of days later, we began to send groups to Bucca. Our squadron was so large that we couldn't all go at once. A small contingent traveled by ground convoy from Kuwait to Bucca; they were transporting all our extra gear and luggage. From this point on, we lived with one uniform and whatever was in our duffel bag, along with all our weapons. The rest of us began to leave in teams of about fifty a day. Again Taylor, TSgt Holmes, and I were split up. They left on the first day, and somehow, I was in one of the last groups. We all promised to meet up as soon as we could once we got to Bucca. Even though I had some other friends to hang out with, I sighed as I watched Taylor and TSgt Holmes leave. I especially missed Taylor; she was my battle buddy. So when she and TSgt Holmes left together, I was suddenly without my battle buddies.

That didn't mean I was alone though; I still lived with more than thirty other women and quickly found some new friends. By this point, almost all of us from Camp McGregor knew each other at least a little. However, we were still getting to know the females from Fort Lewis. I did know Lowell from my first base in Okinawa. The first time I met her was when someone told me how much she and I looked alike. Sure enough, less than five minutes later, she walked by, and I could see what my friend meant. Our appearance was almost exactly the same except her hair was brown and mine was blacker. We joked that the twins were back together again. Now, she would be in QRF too.

I also got to hang out with Chapel. She was petite and quiet, at least until she got to know you. She was also one of the very few females to become a Phoenix Raven, which was a specialized certification for Security Forces. They are trained singularly to go with aircraft into hotspots around the world and provide protection for the aircraft and crews. Most bases have only one or two spots for Ravens, so when a class opened for training, only Security Forces Commanders decide who can apply from their base. Chapel was also National Guard—she had done her initial four-year active-duty enlistment and then joined the Guard afterward. She had to request to deploy and was the only one from her unit deploying. Most of us were on thirteen-man squads from different bases. But Chapel was alone. I highly respected her accomplishments and her courage. We spent quite a bit of time together in Kuwait. Unfortunately, after we got to Bucca, she worked at the opposite end of the TIF, so we rarely saw each other.

On the day I left, a small dust storm quickly blew through. Each day, we had medium-sized dust storms. The day started out sunny, and by dinnertime, the sun was blotted out by a large cloud. We could watch the storm slowly progress toward us since the ground was so flat. Once it hit, the wind swirled dust everywhere. Nothing stopped the sand from covering your entire body, teeth, ears, and eyelashes. Sandstorms stopped almost anything from flying. Too many helicopters had crashed at the beginning of the war due to the whiteout conditions of sandstorms. Thankfully, the day of our flight, we only had a small storm, oddly in the morning.

We were bused up to the Kuwait–Iraq border in one of those huge Kuwaiti luxury buses. The seats were more comfortable than the metal torture racks the Army called cots. Sleep beckoned as soon as the engines started but not for me; my brain raced faster than the speed of light. Excitement and fear fought for domination, knowing that the final destination loomed only a few miles away. I had trained for the TIF, but until I really worked in it, how I would react to the pressure was still unknown. *Would I end up being too weak or indecisive when I needed to make decisions? Would I freeze? What if my mistake got someone killed? Could I live with that?* More sweat trickled down my already-soaked shirt. *Could I measure up?* All military personnel, especially women, are constantly evaluated to see if we are keeping up.

I looked out the windows while I listened to my headphones. As we got closer to the border, there was less and less traffic. Yet more cars were ditched along the road: old rusted cars and trucks, speckled here and there with the skeletons of decrepit tankers and troop vehicles. These vehicles from Desert Storm had just been abandoned here, junked and burned up, left to rot in the desert sun. In fifteen or twenty years, would some other young kid see this same ghost yard, and would our OIF leftovers be just burned junk rotting here too?

We soon arrived at Camp Navistar, a base for the US's entrance into Iraq at the start of the war. We were simply jumping on one of the helicopters for a trip of less than fifteen minutes. But we had to wait until dark for takeoff to minimize the possibility of getting shot at. Yes, I know I joined the Air Force, but I was terrified of flying. I have been in big planes, small planes, and even flown through a typhoon, but I still get jittery and almost sickly nervous getting on a plane. In addition, this was not a plane but a helicopter. I thought I would pass out from fear, but the even greater fear of looking weak held me in check.

As soon as it got dark enough, we prepared to fly out. In order to get on the helicopter, we had to walk to the end, slouch a little, and not get too close to the back rotor, or we'd lose our heads or arms. The helo crew chief explained this while laughing. Nope, I wasn't nervous at all. I was so far beyond nervous—"piss-ass scared" is a better term. But we all got situated safely, and off we flew. All I could see out the window was pitch black. Abruptly, off in the distance was a sprawling mass of concrete brilliantly lit by hundreds of standing lights, my new home-sweet-home. From the air, Camp Bucca actually looked kind of pretty, like a bunch of sparkly lights in a dark sky. Once we were circling over it, the image changed to hundreds of large blinding stadium-type lights; there was no darkness under those lights or beauty either. I didn't know the monsters that were waiting for me down there, and I especially didn't know that one of those monsters would be me.

CHAPTER THREE

THEY'RE HAPPY TO SEE YOU

A s our helicopter began its large, circling arc over the base, we all looked out the windows or the end of the open helo. The rear gunner sat there with his .50-cal machine gun. As we passed over the actual TIF, he yelled to us, "Hey, look outside. The prison is rioting." Some buildings were on fire, but I had no way of knowing which ones.

Someone else asked, "Why are they doing that?"

"They're happy to see you!" The gunner laughed, sounding a lot like the guy from *Full Metal Jacket*. If he had started screaming, "Get some" and shooting the .50-cal, I wouldn't have been too surprised. All through training, many moments made me pause and think, but this was my first true "oh shit" moment. I was assigned to QRF, so situations like this would be my daily routine. What the hell had I gotten myself into?

The minute I got off the helo, the disgusting smell hit me like a putrid wave of sickness. One whiff and I almost gagged at the odor of thousands of sweaty, unclean bodies combined with rotten food and burning trash cans. "What *is* that smell?" I choked out.

One of the guys leading us to the living area said, "It's the prison. It's only this bad because we're close to it. Once we get to the living area, it won't be so bad. Besides, you won't even notice it after a while."

The hell I won't. Even when we got farther away from the prison, the stench didn't abate.

We were escorted from the helo pad by some of the current and soon-to-be leaving SF command element. With all our gear and weapons slung on our backs, it was a nice night for a little mile-long trek over dark and unfamiliar terrain. As an added bonus, my base had sent me with three weapons instead of two: an M9, M4, and M16 with a grenade tube attached; it was a pain in the ass to carry them, but I felt a little like Rambo. Once we reached our SF squadron building, Chief Master Sergeant Mack and the outgoing Chief Master Sergeant had us rally up in an open area.

Chief Mack welcomed us to the camp and said he was trying to finalize our living quarters; he would be handing out assignments in about an hour. The outgoing chief asked if he could address us briefly, and Chief Mack seemed to hesitate for a second before saying yes. (Normally, as equals, the outgoing and incoming Chiefs could freely address incoming troops.) As he began to talk, his raspy voice grated on us. *Too many unfiltered cigarettes, Chief!* I thought. Now it was dark outside and hard to actually see him, but at one point, someone opened the squadron door, and he was directly in the light. My jaw dropped. He had black circles around his eyes, his shoulders slumped, and he just oozed exhaustion and defeated hopelessness. He was leadership, not one of the line troops. If he looked this bad, what would they be like?

I will try to summarize his speech: "Welcome to the most awful place on earth. When you leave here, you will not be the same person. This place is hell. Just remember, don't let the monsters out." That was it: the shortest and most demoralizing speech I've ever heard from a chief. We all stood in shocked silence after he walked away. This was our leadership, the supposed toughest of the tough, and he was broken. *This place is going to kill us or make us kill ourselves.* I began to understand why two Navy guys offed themselves. And what the hell was he talking about? Letting monsters out? What did that mean? Of course, we wouldn't let them out; those detainees were staying in their cages.

Even though that was probably the worst welcome speech I have ever heard, it was honest. He was completely right on every point, and little did I know at the time, the monsters weren't the people we were guarding.

No. He meant the monsters were us.

Five months later, some people from my base at Little Rock arrived. They initially didn't even recognize us. We had changed into totally different people. Hatred and anger had already eaten away some of our spirit. Our outlook on life at Bucca had become so hopeless that it was beginning to reflect in our character and appearance, and that was only halfway through the deployment.

We got our room assignments, and everyone split up to look for their living quarters, which ranged from pretty nice to third-world awful. Some of the lowest-ranking airmen lived for months in tents like what we had in Kuwait. Only here, they were broken down in cot quarters with chip-wood board, about sixty to a tent. Others lived in quads built for four to six guys stuffed with eight to ten. The lower- to mid-level NCOs were either in quads with only four people or a pod with only two people. For once, my luck held out, and I was assigned a pod even though I wasn't actually an NCO yet. In addition, my pod was right around the corner from Taylor and TSgt Holmes, who had managed to secure a pod with each other. My roommate, SSgt Becky Rahn, wasn't actually SF but an orderly room clerk who worked in the Commander's office. She had the first scoop on any and all news about when we got extended, left, mail call, etc. Unfortunately, she never went into the TIF, so she never quite got used to how my uniform smelled after work. Despite that, we became pretty good friends. Even though she wasn't a cop, she was one tough woman; she had done all the pre-deployment training with us with none of the experience of the career field.

Our chain of command included Lt. Col. Shell, our squadron commander; Army Lt. Col. Williams, the TIF commander; and a Navy Captain, whom I really never saw. I didn't even know his name. He was our Living Area (LSA) commander. Usually, when any SF squadrons were deployed, they answered to their squadron commander. But not at Bucca. Once we entered the TIF, we answered to Lt. Col. Williams, who wasn't in the Air Force. Once we returned to the living area, our commander became Lt. Col. Shell who, in turn, answered to the Navy Captain. This was a case of too many Colonels and Lt. Colonels, which resulted in many mixed messages to lower-ranking people. Additionally, Col. Williams and Col. Shell had a few personal issues, so Col. Shell could not see us often while in the TIF. At first, he could come to the larger incidents, but after a while, he was no longer welcome (i.e., kicked out). Since he could not really be around his airmen, his job was that much harder, especially because we didn't understand the situation at all. We took it personally and didn't think he wanted to see us. It wasn't until much later, after the deployment, that I learned of the disagreements between leadership and his frustration with not being around his airmen.

The TIF was very large, a mile north to south and about half a mile east to west. It was the largest detainment facility in the country and continually expanding. There were two gates, a north and south gate with a connecting road. The road was nicknamed "the Mile" from *The Green Mile*, and well, it was a mile long. On either side of the Mile were detainee compounds. Compound 6 was located near the SHU (Special Handling Unit). The SHU was specifically for detainees in isolation, terrorist leaders, known violent criminals, and similar individuals. To give you an idea of how overcrowded the TIF was, Compound 6 was considered overflow for the SHU. In other words, all the detainees in Compound 6 were actually supposed to be in insolation, but there was no room for them. So 6 was broken down into small groups of about twenty–twenty-five detainees per section. Of course, the housing for them only had room for about fifteen–eighteen detainees. So even the overflow was, well, overflowing.

When I started at QRF, our area was directly next to Compound 6. Eventually, we would move to a larger area on the Navy side, mostly because our proximity to Compound 6 meant the detainees were continually pelting stuff at us. One guy almost got knocked out by a piece of concrete while he was headed to the shitter. We had to wear all our gear all the time, which got tiring after a while.

The other compounds were either broken into four quads, housing about 200 to 250 detainees per quad, or compounds that we called communals. In communal compounds, all the detainees (around a thousand or more) were in one large space. These detainees were supposed to be the less-violent criminals, those with supposedly better behavior. We didn't find out what a bad idea this was until later, and we wouldn't have been able to change the setup anyhow. Those compounds had been around a long time before we got there.

Now Compounds 1–6 were on one side while Compounds 7–12 were on the other. We had no Compound 11; that area was the TIF Hospital. Compound 12 was considered a special unit as well; in one part, we housed all the elderly, injured, or wheelchair-bound detainees. The other side held all the underage boys; we had around 150 or more boys ranging from ten to sixteen, and obviously, they couldn't be placed in the adult compounds.

This was all just the Air Force side; on the other side, behind Compounds 7–12, were the Navy Compounds 14–18 (with no Compound 13 as it's an unlucky number). They were only the four quadrant structures; there were no communals. As the TIF's only QRF, we worked on both the Air Force and Navy sides, responding to situations in either area. About seventy of us were on a shift to respond to riots or any unrest in a space that held more than sixteen thousand people with numbers growing daily.

It gets better! Almost immediately after we arrived, we began building even more compounds outside the TIF walls. We had gotten so full that we were forced to build extra compounds, called the Hastys, right next to the perimeter of the base. When I say "we," I mean us AF cops, Army, and Navy people. There were no specialized construction crews, just us.

CHAPTER FOUR

SMELLS LIKE ASS, NOW SO DO I

E very base in Iraq and Afghanistan has a certain smell. It might be where the base is located, like in a city or near the river. The food, forms of cleanliness or lack thereof, the types of bathroom facilities—all these swirl together to create a unique odor at each location. In Pakistan, the overall smell was of burning trash and occasionally bodies. Camp Bucca was no different except it was compounded by the fact that it was a prison as well.

At Bucca, we had a pond between our living area and the prison. This pond was a brownish color when I arrived; it gave off a hint of sewer smell but not too bad. By the time I left, it had turned green with mold growing on top of it. The smell was enough to gag on if we were unlucky enough to walk by it. No one seemed to know the point of the pond; we joked it was where they hid the bodies of escapees. Maybe it was sewage overflow, but I can't be certain.

Inside the TIF, the detainees had wash closet (WC) areas, which were their bathrooms and showers. They were small concrete buildings; the stench of baking shit and rancid piss still makes me gag. In addition, those toilets were never pumped out and were overflowing, so most detainees just went in the dirt outside. I never got used to searching the WCs; most of the time, we took turns because no one could be in there for more than a few seconds without vomiting.

The situation was a little better when we were out at the Hastys; they had Porta Johns that were cleaned every day. But as a tradeoff, the Hastys didn't have closed-off showers, just a row of shower heads in full view of the tower guards. Most detainees just showered with their clothes on, letting the water and soap dry on their clothes and covered areas. So the shit smell was less, but the body funk grew. I blame my addiction to Bath and Body Works on Bucca; I never want to even accidentally smell that place again.

To top the entire issue of smell was our ever-smoking burn pit. It took care of all the trash our base created and then some. Everything was burned in there: sewage, old food, metal, plastic, dead animals, anything that had no use on the base. When we moved to the Hastys, the burn pit was about a hundred yards away. When they stoked it, the heat increased, and whenever the wind blew, which was constantly, our towers were blinded and choked by the black smoke.

A lot of controversy has surfaced over the burn pits and illnesses that many veterans have. No matter the cause, many people have health issues after serving at Camp Bucca, from skin lesions to renal failure to lupus to cancer. These people were in the prime of life and had suddenly developed life-threatening diseases well outside the normal age groups. For example, a thirty-year-old marathon runner was inexplicably diagnosed with renal failure, or a thirty-five-year-old suddenly developed lupus, Grave's disease, and an unknown autoimmune disorder. Something was toxic over there that needs to be acknowledged and addressed by military and Veteran's Affairs leadership. I have been one of the lucky ones; I only get a semi-yearly rash that covers my upper legs and arms. Doctors have no idea what it is, but the only issue so far is the itchiness.

We found out just how bad the air and smell were once we left Bucca. It had literally changed the color of our clothes! Everything we wore there had a yellow-brown tinge that never went away. Even after washing them over and over back home, the color and the faintest smell remained. Bucca had stained our clothes along with our souls.

CHAPTER FIVE
BAPTISM OF FIRE

I woke up for my first day, excited and nervous. I took a quick shower in the closest cadillac, which was hidden around the back corner of my pod. I headed over to the chow hall and grabbed a quick lunch by myself since I didn't know too many people yet. Then I back-tracked to the staging area, our pickup–drop-off point, stopping at a Porta John along the way. Between 1030 and 1135 hours, I had already walked well over a mile. I was trying to gauge roughly how long it took me to get ready so I could establish a morning routine. When working twelve–fourteen hours a day, routines can be crucial in making sure everything gets accomplished. Little did I know that my routine would actually be chaos.

At the staging area, I recognized a few faces from training. Even though we barely knew each other, we now clustered around like old friends. The majority of QRF were either people leaving in less than a week or people that had been there for almost four months. Only a few of us new people had been selected for QRF, and from that few, we had been split between the two shifts. At about 1145 hours, we loaded into a five-ton truck and a deuce-and-a-half truck, and the

NCOs rode in a covered Humvee. Since I was not an NCO yet, I rode with the airmen in the five-ton. Not an easy feat, since the base of the five-ton is approximately six feet high. We could get on in one of two ways: climb a narrow ladder and pull up or climb over the side, using the tires as a ladder. The tires were easier, and the ladder was incredibly narrow. The deuce didn't even have a ladder; it was just pull up or climb over the side. The only way down was a nice, gentle jump off the edge. Add a helmet, flak vest with plates, weapons, and a backpack, and suddenly, the gentle jump became a surefire way for knee and back injuries. I would experience this firsthand; by the time I left Bucca, my right knee and lower back were permanently damaged.

On the ride out, most of us new guys were quiet since we didn't know each other or know what to expect. Once we rounded the road toward the TIF, even the old guys were getting quiet, and the Bucca smell became worse. The growing smell coincided with the dying conversations. Nerves were on edge; not even stupid jokes could cut the stress level. This was another daily routine; we would gradually grow more quiet going to work and slowly get louder the farther away we got from the TIF. Right as we pulled through the gate came shouting, chanting, and the pinging of rocks hitting fences, incredibly familiar sounds in the following months. We reached the QRF station just as the first truck was rolling out. The compound next to us, Compound 6, had initiated a riot right before we arrived.

Once off the five-ton, we scrambled to the armory, where we threw our weapons to the armorer, and she gave us batons and shields. None of us newbies were given shotguns, FN 303s, or the grenades yet; we would need to prove ourselves first. Even though the compound was literally yards away, we had to again climb on the five-ton for the quick ride over.

As we arrived, inside the little twenty-five-man quads, the detainees were flinging rocks, oranges, and milk cartons over the fence. They had ripped apart some of the tents, snapped the metal tent poles in two, and were using them as bats and swords. Those that had wooden caravans instead of tents were chipping away at the wood and flinging chunks of concrete with slingshots. All the while, they were chanting, "Allah Ackbar!" over and over in sing-song voices.

As soon as the truck stopped, we jumped down and hustled into the compound walk area. Immediately, we were hit with oranges and rocks. Our sergeants organized about thirty of us into an entry team with a shield holder in front and baton holder right behind the shield. As we were preparing to move into one of the quads, a guy next to me said, "I have done this shit for six months, and I'm leaving in less than a week. If I get hurt now, I'm gonna be so pissed!"

Then he asked me if I was new. When I said yes, he gave me a golden gem of knowledge. "When you see them throwing either milk cartons or water bottles with white shit in them, keep your mouth shut!" He nicely explained that the detainees would mix rotten milk with sperm and let it sit out in the sun. When riots started, they would fling those at us. We called it man-gurt. Almost immediately after he told me about this lovely concoction, I got a sampling of it on my flak vest and right shoulder. Welcome to Bucca!

After about five minutes, we had enough people to enter the quad. Our mission was to push the detainees into their small holding area, away from their much bigger living area. The holding area was mainly used for conducting a head count or searching their living area. Since Compound 6 was refusing to do their mandatory head count and was instead rioting, we were to force them into the holding area. Our method was to march in and force them from one end of the area to the other and then lock them in. It sounds simple, but it's like herding cats with shivs. Right as we began moving in, I asked the guy next to me, "How do we push them to the end?"

"Easy, the shields just bump them along from one end to the other, and us baton guys smack anyone who resists."

In we swept. The first guy on my side did not bump along the shield, so I began smacking him with the baton. It seemed to work. Hitting someone was a great way to relieve the combination of built-up emotions: fear, nerves, excitement, adrenaline, and more that had built up in my body. Later, I thought, *Hmmm. That shouldn't have been easy. But it was actually a little fun.* We continued pressing forward as one group when, suddenly, my shield and a few others stopped moving. "Push forward!" I yelled.

"I can't! This bastard is pushing me with a damn fence!" my shield holder screamed back. Suddenly, a few shotguns blasted from the tower, and the fence guys scurried back inside their tent. We were outside hitting the detainees—I don't really remember how long, but it was effective—and we left a few laying on the ground. My arm was swinging on its own, powered by a thrill of energy and enjoyment. Crack! A groan and a body fell. *I could do this all day.*

As a group, we headed to the tent. We stepped inside, and for a second, we were incredibly disoriented because there was no light. We started fighting detainees and beating them to go back outside. Over the horrible, awful stench of the TIF, a lovely aroma of a campfire began to waft. The smell of s'mores, church cookouts, and roasting hotdogs all crowded in with chaos, shit, and screaming men. I was starting to sweat like crazy. Even in February, southern Iraq gets pretty warm during the day. Plus, with all the adrenaline and chaos going on, my clothes were rapidly collecting salt stains. But sweat was now running into my eyes and burning like crazy, and that campfire smell was growing. Suddenly, a hand on my flak vest jerked me back; my right hand never left my shield's flak vest, so she flew back with me too. Everyone was screaming for our group to get out; as we did, I glanced up at the roof. The assholes lured us into the tent and snuck out the back while setting it on fire. I knew they hated us, but this was the first time I realized they actually wanted to kill us. They looked directly into my eyes and wanted me dead; I had never experienced that level of hatred before.

But I was a quick student, and I soon felt the same about them. Thankfully, one of the last people entering the tent looked up and saw the flames. One part of our training was successful; we were trained to *never* ever let go of the vest of the person in front of you; lose your hand if you have to, but holding that vest could save their life. That day, it did. We pulled back out of the tent and engaged the fence pole detainees again. Finally, we pushed them into the holding area. Then we headed over to the next quad and did it again. On the other side, another team was doing the exact same thing.

After a while, the detainees became less resistant; the majority of them were locked down, and so there were fewer to antagonize each other. This does not mean they were compliant, only that there were fewer of them. As we prepared to enter yet another area, a sergeant came by with a huge can of mace the size of a fire extinguisher. It operated on the same principle: point at detainee, aim nozzle, and fire. The result was instant: Where six or seven detainees were previously rioting, suddenly there were none. They ran from that spray like the devil, but too bad for them, the spray shot out about forty-five feet. They all got plastered, and a few of us did too. But our pepper-spray training kicked in, and we could fight our way through the mace fog; pepper spray coupled with anger pushed me to finish the job. We should have used it before we shielded, smashed, and kicked our way through four areas.

As we were getting ready to go to the next area, someone said, "We need to get that guy. He looks like he's having a bad reaction to the spray." I turned, fully expecting to see a military member. Instead, a detainee was lying on the ground inside the quad, gasping for air and clutching at his chest. I turned away to go to the next area, thinking the guy wasn't serious about helping him until the riot died down. But he was completely serious. The next thing I know, I was told to help remove the guy from the living area. Now the area hadn't been cleared, and they wanted us to go save some asshole that had been actively trying to harm us not five minutes ago. *Screw this guy!* I thought as I went in with three others to pick him up. Not a single one of us wanted to do this, and as we began carrying him, he was still chanting and calling us infidels.

Once we cleared the main fence as a group, we dumped him on the ground and walked off. Mr. We-Have-To-Save-Him got stuck doing all the rest of the work of dragging him to a Humvee and driving him to the TIF hospital. I couldn't wrap my mind around what we had just done. Even in combat, you wait until everything has calmed down before taking care of enemy combatants. The injustice of putting people in extra danger to help a guy who wanted us dead made me far angrier than any mace could. Deep inside me, the monster began to growl.

Within thirty minutes, the majority of the riot was done. QRF was cleared to go back to their area while Compound 6 staff did their head counts and cleaned up. We no longer had a ride back to our area. The off-going shift needed the vehicles to go back to the LSA, so we walked. Four hours done in my first shift, only eight-to-ten more left. I had already learned an important lesson: Always bring an extra DCU top. For the rest of the day, I was stuck with a sweaty, stinky, man-gurt-stained top. But on a positive side, now that I was totally immersed in funk, the Bucca stench all but disappeared. As the adrenaline rush of the first few hours began to fade, I couldn't figure out why my arm was so sore. I thought I had maybe swung my baton a few times; in reality, I had been hitting people with it for almost an hour. Time truly becomes fluid when adrenaline spikes; I had no idea who, where, or how many people I hit that morning. It should have bothered me, but it didn't.

For the rest of the shift, we spent time getting to know each other and learning about some of our cool gear. We had a REV 113—it looks like a miniature tank complete with the track and cool turret.[1] We also had our very own firetruck. Yes, the base proper had a fire department that responded to TIF fires, but ours was distinctly for the purpose of hosing large amounts of detainees as they rioted. It could be quite effective. We affectionately named her Christine, like the car from the horror movie.

In our armory, we had less-than-lethal shotguns and ammunition. We also had a weapon called a FN 303. It's like a paintball gun with the power and velocity cranked up about a hundred times. The paintballs were also harder than regular ones; they were encased in hardened plastic with small pieces of shaved bismuth attached to the end for maximum impact. All towers in the TIF had these, and most of the rovers did too. These shot way farther than a regular paintball gun, no one shot them back at you, and they could blind people if you aimed them just right.

The armory also had stinger grenades; some were filled with pellets and others with OC. The OC grenades had to be used carefully because if the wind changed directions that cloud would fall back on us. That happened many times. Now all these weapons were designed to be not deadly; however, with any weapon, the possibility of lethal force would happen, at least occasionally.

We all got a chance to meet our flight members and flight sergeants. TSgt V was part of the group that had already been at Bucca for about four months. He wasn't given to a lot of talking, but he could be surprisingly loud when he needed to be. Our other flight sergeant was TSgt Ewing. He was new to Bucca, but I hadn't really done any training with or around him. He was also pretty quiet but was good at looking out for his people. And if we got stuck somewhere for a stupidly long amount of time, both our flight sergeants made sure that they were there with us, no matter what kind of shit we were dealing with. They never asked us to do anything they wouldn't do. I saw them search detainees, dig holes, and get smacked with rocks, feces, and everything else.

QRF had quite a few SSgts who were in charge of elements or squads. Each squad rotated different housekeeping duties: sweep, mop, trash, etc. We also rotated who went to get chow. There was SSgt Bird, a young guy, newly married and totally devoted to his wife. He was huge and into weightlifting and had gained like forty-five pounds of muscle mass. SSgt Ash was an awesome dude, quick to make a joke, and he would sometimes attempt to get the detainees to smile. SSgt Crosby was a complete badass with the pepper spray cans. She was the one who had blasted the detainees at Compound 6. She grabbed two cans, one in each hand, and walked down the walkway with a huge smile, just spraying the hell out of them. As to SSgt Eliza Orleans, there is no adequate description for her. The first time I met her, she seemed to vibrate with the enjoyment of life. She had her own problems at Bucca like we all did, but I never—not once—saw her down or upset. The only exception was at the very end of their deployment, which was totally understandable. She became and has stayed one of my closest friends.

My element leader was SSgt Young. He was quiet at first, but man, he had a quick humor that you had to look out for. As the ranking Senior Airman (Staff Select) in the squad, he made it clear that once we had settled into our jobs, I would be the one taking charge of the element's day-to-day activities. In short, I would make sure they had all their gear and did all the housekeeping when it was our turn. I would bring up any more serious issues with him. Our element rounded out with SrA Melendez, A1C Copeland, A1C Sullivan, and A1C Caldwell. I was responsible for trying to keep these people safe, which was a little overwhelming. That was a lot of responsibility at only twenty-two. I didn't lightly dismiss it.

With the exception of Caldwell, all of my element were from the two-hundred-man November team that was scheduled to leave in

May. That first riot seemed to immediately unite our two teams. Usually, teams who arrive at different times have a rough time at the beginning and struggle to blend. But the cohesion between our two groups—the November group and our January group—was almost immediate. At times, I couldn't keep track of who had gotten to Bucca when. To their credit, the older group welcomed and taught us without complaint.

Later that night, when I got back to my pod, as soon as I walked in, SSgt Rahn said, "Phew, O'Brien, you stink!"

I looked at her and grinned. "SSgt Rahn, I had a great day!" We talked about the riot and all the craziness; I still became angry when I told her about the stupidity of carrying that one detainee. That situation was probably an isolated issue with a stupid NCO; I was sure it wouldn't happen again. We were taught to always take care of our people first; that guy must have been some shithead looking for a medal. I was certain our leadership would take care of us. Although there was now a little hesitation in my certainty; if one guy was like that, maybe there were more. But I tried to shake off my anger at my own people.

The only thing Rahn and I ever disagreed on was the fact that I always called her SSgt Rahn. She would bug me over and over to just call her Becky, but I never did. In my career field, we rarely called anyone by their first names, and only SSgts or above called each by just their last name. The habit was much too ingrained in me.

As to living arrangements, we had the perfect schedule. She worked from 0900 to 2100, and I from 1200 to 2400, so each of us had a few hours to ourselves either before or after work. It's important to have some time alone and damn near impossible to do that on a deployment. A balance was necessary; a little alone time was good, too much and weird shit begins to run through your head.

For the next couple of days, the routine was the same: wake up, shower, eat, go to work, have a riot, finish the shift, come to the pod.

On maybe the third or fourth night, I woke up to the base alarm going off. Rahn and I both started getting dressed and geared up. We were really confused because neither of us had heard any explosions, so once we were all ready, we had no idea where to go. As the siren blasted in between alarms, a message was blaring. "Operation Dar—." The rest was indecipherable. So we started guessing based on the sound: operation Darrin, Darfur, Darth Vader ... We started cracking up as we made up different names.

Suddenly, one of my guys, Sullivan, from QRF banged on our door. "O'Brien! Don't you hear the Dartmoore? Hurry up, you need to be at the rally area for patrol!"

I asked, "What the hell is a Dartmoore?"

He explained to both of us that Operation Dartmoore was the code given when detainees escaped. We should have been briefed about this at our in-processing, but because people were leaving too fast, we had to go to work immediately and missed days of briefings. How could leadership not tell us about something this important? Suddenly, everything wasn't hilarious anymore; the monster inside began to growl louder.

I arrived at the staging area, and we were sent out to different parts of the base; some went to the TIF area, and some went to the LSA. We weren't given any fun little batons or less-than-lethal weapons this time; once a detainee escaped, we shot to kill. This was by far the scariest work: searching empty tents, looking in areas with little to no light, and trying to find some guy that would simply love to kill you as an offering to Allah before he died. We were in the process of building new compounds outside the TIF, and those areas had to be searched first. They didn't have any electricity; we just used our flashlights. *Now I know how the mom in* The Shining *felt.* In those half-finished compounds, I learned that fear has a smell. I never knew if I wanted to catch the detainee or if I hoped someone else did, because even though they usually surrendered, they usually put up a fight before they were captured. After about three hours of prowling around, we were released back to our area and expected to report for work about four hours later.

I wish I could say this was the only time we had an escape attempt, but in reality, we easily had at least thirty or more attempts over the next nine months. None of the detainees were gone for too long. Some made it off base; some got lost and were caught in different areas of the base. Only one guy was never found. This was as the majority of us were still arriving from Kuwait; Taylor's compound was missing a guy from one of their quads. Operation Dartmoore was activated, and people searched for hours. QRF was pulled in to the quad to dig around the sleeping areas and look for a possible tunnel. Dogs were brought in to track, all the prison's trash bags were ripped open, but nothing was found. The only thing notable was a small cup of blood near the guy's bed mat. He must have done something really bad to piss off the others to the point they would kill him and hide the body. Normally, when detainees beat and killed each other, they didn't bother to try to hide the body. Personally, I think they cut him up and put him in the hand-dug toilets. The amount of shit and sludge in those would have quickly consumed him. Between Dartmoores, mortar attacks, rocket attacks, and riots at all hours, we were constantly running on four hours or fewer of sleep. I hadn't expected to get much sleep on deployment, but the lack of sleep showed me the stark reality of Bucca, especially when compared with home.

---

1. On each corner of the 113, there was a less-than-lethal claymore mine. When it exploded, it would shoot hundreds of little rubber pellets all over. "Less than lethal" is a term given to any weapon when the primary function is not to kill but maim. Don't be fooled, it can be and, at times, was still very lethal.

CHAPTER SIX

A HOSPITAL VISIT

A fter about two weeks, we finally worked out a rotation schedule so that everyone could have a day off. On my first day off, I slept in later than usual, until around 0700, which I needed. I had been quite sick since training at McGregor, and being in riots with a lot of smoke and fire hadn't helped any. After I ate, I headed over to the medical tent to get checked out. I waited for almost two hours just for a cold-pack. The little Lt. Physician's Assistant just said I had the newcomer's crud, and I should suck it up and get over it. (Newcomer's crud is the sickness everyone gets when arriving at their deployed station, regardless of where that is. It is a result of a dramatic change in weather, trash burning, and exposure to everyone else and is so named because, well, new people are the ones who get it.) I had explained that I knew it wasn't newcomer's crud since I had been sick since McGregor. No matter, he was done, and I had to leave.

I took the stupid cold-pack filled with a few Motrin, a couple of cough drops, and some Kleenex and headed back out. I quickly called my parents to tell them I was alive and made it to Iraq. (By now, I had already been there for two weeks but hadn't been able to call sooner.)

Later, I was actually feeling better, so I went to the gym for a workout. Afterward, I grabbed dinner and headed back to my pod.

I was a little tired, so I decided to go to bed early and get some extra sleep before work the next day. I grabbed my cough syrup, which I had been chugging since McGregor, took a couple of sips, and laid down. The next thing I heard was someone banging on my door. I staggered over, punch-drunk (from the medicine and my deep sleep) and let my buddy Taylor in. She had just gotten off work and was coming to hang out for a little bit. We chatted for a bit, and then we headed to the latrine cadillac. I was still feeling a bit woozy and wasn't fully awake. What comes next is a mixture of my memory and what others have told me. As we were walking, suddenly my vision narrowed in on the back of Taylor's head. *My eyes don't work. Come on, open up!* Dinner started backtracking up my throat as the world teetered around me; this only happened when I was really drunk, which I wasn't. I stopped and leaned against a barrier.

Taylor turned toward me. "Are you all right? You don't look so hot."

All I got out was, "I don't feel so—" Bam! I crashed right onto the rocks!

The next thing I remember was being incredibly comfortable except something was smacking me. Slowly, my hearing tuned in. "Heather! Heather! Wake up!" Taylor kept yelling over and over.

I mumbled, "Leave me alone." My body was so relaxed on the pillowy cushions. I was in bliss.

"Are you fucking kidding me? Is this a joke? Answer me!"

Now I was confused. Was *what* a joke? And why was it so hard to talk? Finally, I managed to croak out, "What joke?"

Taylor asked me where I was; I told her I was sleeping in my pod. Eventually, I woke up enough to open my eyes. Except I was not in bed but lying on some rocks. All her yelling had attracted the attention of my roommate, Rahn. Our medical tent was closed, and only the TIF hospital, which was over a mile away, was open overnight. I could barely stay awake sitting; no way was I walking a mile! Rahn ran to the squadron office and got permission (I think) to use the Commander's golf cart to transport me to the TIF. She couldn't go with us because she didn't have a TIF badge and would not be allowed in. So they loaded me up and off we went—Taylor with one hand on the wheel and another gripping me so I wouldn't fall out. (Even so, I almost did a few times.) What a beautiful night in Iraq, wind tickling my face, arms too dead to brush my hair aside. We were wildly driving over pot-holed roads, but my body was Jell-O and absorbed each shock. Two blinks later, we were screeching up to the front of the TIF hospital. *Amazing! When did we go through the security check?* Taylor strained her wrist and forearm because I couldn't even hold my head up.

Once in the hospital, the team had a hard time putting an IV in me because apparently, I was extremely dehydrated. The medic tried to put a needle in at a 90-degree angle, which should never happen; needles go in at a 15-to-20-degree angle! The last person to attempt the IV was a little shaky. So Taylor grabbed my hand and just told me to look away. As the fluids started doing their job and I began waking back up, I looked around at three or four detainees in beds around me. They weren't speaking, but they stared at us, their eyes a bottomless pit. I wanted out of there as fast as possible. Taylor never left me for a second.

After pumping me full of three bags of fluids and giving me some watered-down Gatorade for the road, they released me to go back to the LSA. They finally told me that I didn't have the newcomer's crud but had bronchitis. Even so, I didn't need to miss work, so after about six hours of rest, which for anyone who has been filled up on IV fluids means pissing for those six hours straight, I headed back to work. I actually slept on the toilet; it was easier than trying to walk a quarter of a mile each way to my pod.

I did eventually recover but not without permanent issues. I have gotten bronchitis at least once or twice a year for the last fifteen years. I wasn't the last person to be told by the LSA medical people to "suck it up." One friend was incredibly sick, and thankfully, an Army medic, again in the TIF, caught and recognized the symptoms: meningitis. But to the LSA medics, he was malingering—they almost killed him. Another time, SSgt Bird told them he was having problems using the bathroom, and he thought he might have a kidney stone. Again, he was told to stop whining until he collapsed at work, and the TIF hospital realized he was in renal failure. It's a miracle they didn't actually kill anyone. The detainees received obvious preferential treatment from doctors that actually gave a damn compared to our obviously low-rate mediocre-at-best doctors in the LSA. These issues enraged many of us. Why were suspected terrorists being given preferential treatment over military personnel? Everywhere I looked, I was seeing it more and more. The monster inside was now starting to roar.

CHAPTER SEVEN

I SHOT HIS EYE OUT AND OTHER POWER TRIPS

We went to several riots—I'm not sure how many—before we (the newbies) were finally allowed to start carrying riot guns. The first time I carried the shotgun, probably about two or three weeks after our first riot, we were at Compound 16. We were old riot vets by now, a smooth, well-oiled QRF machine. But here, we encountered a new scenario: The detainees had started making formations. In the movie *300*, all the Spartans used their shields in the front, sides, and over their heads; that is what these guys were doing with their bed mattresses. Every time we shot at them, the riot rounds just ineffectively bounced off the mattresses. Even worse, they also had fence posts and sharpened instruments jutting from the front of their formation, and they were rapidly approaching the fence where we were. The fence was a last resort and blockade; if they reached it and started popping it, they would create an opening for more than 350 of them to break out of. We would be in sudden hand-to-hand fighting.

Pops, our Flight Master Sergeant (MSgt), was on the line that night. His nickname had been given to him because he was constantly calling all of us "kids" and because this was his last deployment; he had extended his service time to finish this one last tour before retirement. He was probably about forty, but in the military world of eighteen- to twenty-five-year-olds, that made him ancient. Normally, Pops was really laid back, smoking and joking with everyone. But tonight, he was livid—his kids were seconds away from hand-to-hand combat and possible death. He grabbed a stinger grenade and tossed it perfectly over the fence, and no shit, it rolled right under the mattresses of that group. No MLB pitcher could have thrown a better pitch. *Bam*! Mattresses and bodies flew apart and up into the sky!

We all started whooping and hollering until nice and relaxed Pops screamed, "What are you waiting for? Shoot the motherfuckers!" And boy, did we ever shoot. Now that the mattresses had been blown apart, it was like a turkey shoot. I had grabbed a whole bunch of the crowd rounds for my shotgun; I didn't like how ineffective the point rounds were, so I only loaded crowd rounds. From the sounds and pellets flying everywhere, I wasn't the only one to use them either. Because the detainees had been using their mattresses, they were closer to the fence than normal—really close for those crowd rounds, which will do some serious damage at close ranges. They did that night—no one died, but at least five detainees lost eyes. The phrase "less than lethal" is just nice words. When a face gets pellet-peeled or an eye shot out, in that moment, most people would rather be dead.

Two things stood out about this riot. 1) We were trained to always be professional and to never yell, hoot, or holler during riots. I never realized how hard that would be with the adrenaline rush, noises, and nonstop action. Every detainee that was shot or knocked down was one less who could attack us. Every synapse was snapping; I didn't even realize that I was the one screaming war cries until later. This solidified my love affair with adrenaline. It began in the first riot but bloomed that night. Later—much later—this wouldn't be too much of an issue; riots eventually became monotonous. 2) It was easy to pull the trigger; I probably shot four or five rounds before I realized I was actually shooting and hitting detainees. These weren't lethal rounds per se, and I'm not equating riots with combat. But this was the first time I had ever had to use a firearm in the line of duty, and I had thought it would be more momentous. In reality, all my training kicked in: aim, breathe, trigger squeeze, and repeat. I was actually a little let down at the lack of emotion. I didn't realize it then, but I was becoming the embodiment of hate. I was allowing hatred and anger to run my thought processes, reactions, and most of my life.

In mid-March, we began to hear rumors of an extension, which wasn't surprising for my group. Most of us had figured that we would be extended a month or two—it was normal in Security Forces deployments. But the older crew was already approaching the beginning of the end of their deployment. They had already been extended once before we arrived. Their group had arrived in November 2006 and was supposed to leave in May 2007; that was with their first extension. Our commander called a quick Commander's Call; only off-duty personnel had to attend. He confirmed the extension of our group to July 2007, but the November crew was still set to leave in May. It sucked but wasn't shocking.

We had also heard other rumors too, rumors of some kind of troop surge in Iraq that was supposed to break the Iraqi resistance. At this point, the guys building additional compounds outside the TIF began working around the clock to finish them. This confirmed our concern; more troops would be needed to manage more compounds, and apparently, someone was expecting us to have our own little surge of detainees. Awesome. We were already overcrowded and would get even more people.

Almost immediately, our in-processing numbers started increasing. Before March, we typically received 100–125 detainees three times a week from Camp Cropper; at the beginning of the Surge, we started receiving 250 or more detainees three times a week.

Our in-processing procedure was quite simple. As the new detainees, shackled and cuffed, were offloaded from the buses, they were placed in Zone 1. They were lined up in rows outside. A row at a time was brought into a shack where the detainee was searched (clothed), the cuff and shackles were removed, and they were zip-cuffed with evil little tight plastic cuffs. The extra-long ends of the zip ties had to be cut off, or detainees would use them to get out of the zip cuffs. They were then walked around the back to another shack where they were fingerprinted and their retinas scanned. This area was also where the Iraqi Correctional Officers (ICOs) searched the detainees' Quran. We had the most issues here as the detainees hated the ICOs and often refused to allow them to touch their Quran. A little zap with a Taser ensured compliance and was much better than pepper spray in an enclosed area. That happened once, we all got gassed; from then on, we only used Tasers and batons in the shacks. After all this, the detainees then moved to Zone 4 where they were again placed outside in rows. Here, they were finally allowed a bottle of water and the opportunity to use the bathroom.

It was normal for about twenty of us to in-process more than 250 detainees. We were walking in small fenced areas with them and nothing but a baton or Taser. We could never let them see us uncertain or afraid. I was quickly learning that detainees often tried to be difficult and intimidating, especially with females. The key was to be a bigger bitch than they were. I was relishing that challenge more and more; the monster inside me was growing. I tried to be in Zone 4 as often as possible so I could show every one of them coming in that I had absolutely no fear but only hatred for them. Rules of engagement were very clear in Zone 4; the guard never had to repeat themselves. If we did, we immediately reinforced our words with a Taser or a baton hit. Violence was very common, and we always had to be more violent than the detainees. Some people favored a quick smack to the offender, but I preferred group punishment so that the person was further punished by his own people later. Some of the ways detainees hurt each other in the compounds were beatings, rapes, and electric torture. I took a secret glee, knowing that even though I never touched the detainee, their pain was of my own making.

One day, A1C Sullivan pointed out a particular young man. "Make sure he does trash. He's got a shitty mouth and attitude." So when trash pickup time came around, I found another guy, and I pointed out the young man and told them they both had to pick up the trash.

The young guy, who was probably between nineteen and twenty-two, looked me dead in the face. "I don't pick up trash, you whore-dog infidel."

Game on! "You're going to do the trash, or else everyone will sit here until you do." It was March, but we were in southern Iraq, so it was a lovely 95 degrees during the day with a sharp cold drop at night. A couple of other detainees volunteered to take his spot, but I wouldn't let them. I was relishing the almost absolute power I had over them. The ability to force them to do what we said was intoxicating. We sat there for over an hour in the heat of the day. Now I was being very nice and giving them all the water they wanted, which created more trash to pick up and a need to piss. That's when I cut off permission to go to the bathrooms. Full bladders in the 90-degree temperatures. You can just imagine. All I had to do was wait until someone pissed themselves, and then the group would turn on this kid. The older men in the group started saying stuff to him in Arabic. I wasn't certain what they said, but it didn't sound pretty.

I went back over to him. "Are you ready to do your new job, Trash-boy?" If he could have killed me, he would have truly enjoyed it, but I was the winner of that power contest. He picked up the trash and threw it away.

As we walked him back to his new compound, he kept glaring at me, and every time, I stared right back and laughed. Once we got to his compound, I told the sergeant the story about why we were so late and how this one was a troublemaker. As I turned to leave, he spit on the ground and called me an infidel again. I just laughed and told him I would see him around. Ironically, I did see him quite a few more times. When his compound started rioting, every time we showed up, I almost always ended up near his quad and seeing him. My most satisfying moment was during one riot where he chucked a piece of granite at me, and I hit him with a shotgun blast to the stomach. It was truly a hate-hate relationship between Trash-boy and me.

In-processing could be a little difficult because whether new or returning, the detainees were pissed. I was prepared for that; of course, they were angry. I would be too if I were going to prison. But surprisingly, the most difficult times we had at processing were at out-processing. A detainee was leaving Bucca for one of three reasons:

1. He was being transferred back to Camp Cropper for court or trial and would probably come back a couple of weeks later.
2. He was being released. Shockingly, not many were happy about this. Upon release, the detainee was turned over to the Iraqi Police who were supposed to take him home. Supposedly, they would take the man into the desert and tell his family to meet them with money in thirty minutes, or they would kill him. At the time, I hoped it was true.
3. The final reason for leaving was the detainee's trial was done and he had gotten a death sentence. The poor bastard would go to Camp Cropper or the Iraqi Police to be executed.

During out-processing, we had a list with each detainee's name, and we checked it very thoroughly. Each name had an identifier for court, release, or execution. The detainees might be terrorists, but they weren't stupid; family members were telling them that people who had gotten released weren't showing up at home. So out-processings were so difficult because the detainees were all convinced they were going to die. I didn't mind the extra violence because I knew they were doing it out of fear. As the deployment got longer and I became more animalistic, I smiled as I looked into the detainee's eyes while checking their names. I was genuinely happy because I knew he was going to die, and I knew it before he did.

"Sargent, Sargent, me free!" That shout was followed by a zap from a Taser and a teenager crying. Yet another kid had decided to play stupid and take off their zip ties, only to find that once they did, we treated them like adults. With almost two hundred kids being out-processed at once, it felt a little like some type of sick twilight zone. Line them up, zip-tie them, see them break the zip tie and walk around, Taser them, make them cry, repeat.

These kids would as soon kill us if given a chance. They hadn't been arrested for just being out past curfew; they were the cellphone holders and snitches of the insurgency. These baby terrorists would boast about calling in troop movements to their elders to watch coalition forces be attacked. It was hard to feel bad for a youth that had gleefully plotted convoy routes for insurgents and helped them set the bombs.

The only reason they were separated from the adults was because it was a prison and some men there would've raped them if given the opportunity. Also, somewhere in the chain of command, some general probably thought that if they were separated from the adults, they might be able to learn the ideals of democracy and freedom. That was a joke. These kids were just as hardened as their parents and grandparents; that's just how Iraq is. Anyhow, higher ups actually built an education center, and now we were tasked with out-processing all the little shitheads in one night and sending them to this new center.

The processing was a nightmare. If I thought the adults were difficult, the little fuckers showed up with a new level of assholeish-ness! The adults wanted to get all the processing done and over with —not these fuckers, nope, they wanted to embrace every part of the adventure. This apparently included pushing our buttons just for fun, which was a very bad idea. If we had done this out-processing earlier in the deployment, we might have treated them a little differently, but by that point, we had been through too many riots, escapes, mortars, and loss. We treated them just like we would adults who misbehaved.

In the separate juvenile compound, their guards had not been easygoing, but they also weren't especially mean either. QRF had only been over there once a month or so for the occasional search or dig. We had more pressing matters to attend to at other compounds. So when these kids were dropped off for their out-processing, they thought we would be the same as the guys they dealt with every day. Wrong. We didn't usually deal with detainees except in riots or processings when they massively outnumbered us in small enclosed areas. We gave one command, and if they didn't comply, we punished them accordingly.

These kids were escape artists when it came to their handcuffs. Their wrists were very small, so the cuffs just slipped right off many of them. Others managed to manipulate their wrists and get out of the ties. One exceptionally dumb kid slipped his ties, walked up behind SSgt Young, and tapped his shoulder. Smooth as could be, SSgt Young lifted him right up and over his shoulder, slammed him into the ground, put his boot on the kid's back, and zip-tied him again. It took that kid nearly a minute to realize what happened. Another little sweetheart decided to try to choke one of the ICOs. After he slipped out of his cuffs, he jumped up and grabbed the ICO by the throat. The ICO kneed the kid in the stomach and, once he let go, began repeatedly slapping him. We actually had to remove the ICO, but we let him slap the kid for a bit first.

We had incidents like this happen all the time during out-processing. Their defiant little cries of "death to America" were rapidly drowned out by their screams as they were tasered or hit. Even today, I sometimes mistake children's noises at play for those screams. By the time we were finished, most of us had declared a hatred of Iraqi children and hoped the education center was some form of work camp. We said this to soothe the sick feeling that we may have slipped into a new level of evil; we were now the people who beat children. Even to this day, when I hear about the poor Iraqi children, I remember those boys, and nothing about them was poor or innocent at all.

CHAPTER EIGHT

BOOM! DEATH

Death-filled hate stares shot thru the fence and tried to cut my throat out. Hundreds, at times, thousands, of men scowled at me with murder written across their faces. Every person that's ever worked at Bucca knows that same feeling. It's so blatant, it's almost palpable. Hate has a vibe that singes the air. In this case, there were about four hundred of them and forty of us, so their expressions spoke volumes.

We were in the middle of a dig and search at yet another compound. The riots had slowed down to the point that we knew they were plotting more, but they were apparently not ready yet. In between almost nightly work duties and ongoing escape attempts, most of us were getting worn down. Personally, I liked doing digs. Our whole job was to tear the living area of a compound apart with picks, shovels, and such. It's hard and hot work but better than the searches. During searches, we would still dig around the outside, but the primary focus was inside the detainees' living quarters. I had successfully gotten used to the smell in the LSA, TIF, and the smoke pit but not their living quarters. Twenty-five–thirty men sleeping in a tent made for ten was not a Bath and Body Works–scented place!

So while we dug and looked for signs of tunneling, the detainees observed us. They glared at us, many times giving us death signals: the finger slashed across the neck, a foot-stomped thumbs up (which in their culture, means "fuck you!"), and such. They also tried to keep tabs on where we were, and if we started getting too close to important items, they tried to break out of their holding area or rioted to stop us from getting too much contraband. I was so excited the first time I found a cache of rocks to use for a riot—until I found out that there were literally hundreds of other caches and different kinds of riot weapons. We would never be able to find all the weapons. They were never-ending, and searching became quite discouraging.

Around the halfway point of our dig, a soft *boom* echoed in the distance. Everyone paused for a moment. It was too far away for the base to call it a valid mortar attack, but still, we paused just to make sure. After a few minutes of quiet and no loud alarm, we continued with our work. That night, we headed home to the LSA, chatting about our plans for the night. I was headed to chow and then the phones. My birthday was just a few days away, and I was hoping to talk to my parents because one never knew what a day would bring. I figured I'd rather be safe than sorry and get my call in as soon as I could.

After quickly dropping off my gear in my pod, I headed to the chow hall, hoping to eat before they shut down. I was walking quite fast, and when I didn't see anyone playing on the basketball court or hanging out near the hookah lounge, I wondered about it but really didn't pay any attention. I made it to the chow hall with minutes to spare, grabbed whatever food was left, and sat down with a few guys from QRF.

The second I sat down, I knew something was wrong. The guys

had serious expressions and talked quietly, which we rarely did. I asked what was going on. One of them asked if I remembered that odd boom earlier in the day, which, of course, I did. Eliza said an IED had hit one of our convoys. Someone had died, but nobody was quite sure who yet. The people in that convoy were still in debriefing. Suddenly, this deployment got deadly serious. Yes, these people wanted to kill us, but I hadn't really thought about that until now. Now someone had died—now some family was about to get the worst news possible. I left the chow hall and headed straight to my pod; I was no longer in any mood to talk about or celebrate my birthday.

The next morning, we were informed of the death of SPC Christopher Young of Company C, 3rd Battalion, 160th Infantry Regiment. He was riding with a mixed group of Army National Guard and Air Force Security Forces on a night patrol. When the convoy crossed a certain bridge, his truck went one way and the Air Force truck went the other way. His side had a bomb; theirs didn't. That's how it was, a roll of the dice every day. He was twenty years old. I didn't know SPC Young, but I went to his memorial service. He isn't forgotten.

When an incident that results in injury or death occurs at a base, the military goes into a blackout mode. This means no communication with people back home—no email, no phone calls, and no letters—until the military can reach the service member's family and notify them about what happened. This meant no calling my family until a couple of days after my birthday. My mom asked me why I hadn't called on my birthday, and I kept trying to be vague about it. But she could be persistent, so finally I just told her that someone died. I added that I didn't know him, that it wasn't in the TIF, and told her not to worry, that it was totally safe where I was. Yes, the last one was a lie, but how would telling the truth have helped her? She was thousands of miles away, and she only would have worried more. A curious thing began to occur after this; days only stood out when something big happened, like a death or major riot. The other days just began to blend together; days, weeks, even months didn't really hold meaning, and even the holidays were a blur.

CHAPTER NINE

ENEMIES ALL AROUND

I 'll give the detainees some credit; they were pretty inventive when it came to making weapons. Of course, they made the traditional toothbrush shanks, but they could make a weapon out of almost anything. They created David-and-Goliath slingshots. They would use the stretchy part from the waistband of their pants along with additional clothing pieces. They could fire a rock at us with deadly accuracy. One of them hit a tower guard who was wearing eye gear and a helmet right above the glasses and right below the helmet. It was a perfect shot. He suffered a crushed nasal passage and cracked skull and was in a coma for several days.

They didn't have a lot of rocks in the compounds; they made them. They took the serving of chai (hot tea we had to give them with their meals) and poured it over bowls and buckets of sand. As it cooled, they formed the mixture into rocks and let them harden. I took two of these rocks home from Iraq; in the six years I had them, they never cracked or crumbled. Not a single piece of them broke off.

Many times, they also used the chai to strengthen the walls of the tunnels they built. These tunnels ranged in size from single person to multiple people who fit in them at once. We found tunnels ranging from just a few feet to over a mile long. Almost every time, the tunnels were headed straight toward our living area, never outside the TIF.

When the riots started getting extra crazy, we began seeing new rocks. Instead of formed by hand, these were poured into orange juice cartons. As the mixture started to harden, they put nails and pieces of the fence through it, making a lethal rock full of metal.

They had no problem taking apart their wooden huts for added materials. We found beat sticks, pieces of wood from the huts smoothed into flat bats complete with a handle. Sometimes during searches, we found homemade restraints made from clothing and hung over one of the beams. Occasionally, they would rewire the A/C unit to make electroshock therapy. Obviously, these weapons weren't made for the guards. Day or night, up in a tower, the screams of detainees torturing each other filled the air. We could easily dehumanize people who were willing to brutalize the guy sleeping next to them.

My personal favorite was the flaming oranges. At one point in Compound 2, a chemist created a way to coat the oranges with some type of film that made them flammable. During riots, these oranges on fire were flung everywhere like old-fashioned catapults. That same chemist created a way to take some of the acidity out of the orange and make a type of acid that burned you if you accidentally touched it. They poured it over some of their weapons and left them in the open for us to find. Thankfully, only two or three people were burned before we realize it was a ploy.

In a weird way, I could understand and almost respect their hatred of us. If some people came from another country into my country and tried to force their ideologies onto me, I would fight them too. But I could not understand how they hated each other so much. At one point, there were more than twenty thousand detainees and a maximum of five thousand military personnel; if they would have worked together, they would have overtaken us. That's a scary thought.

In the TIF, we allowed the detainees to keep hating each other over minor differences. The theory was if the detainees were always fighting each other, then they wouldn't have time to fight us. It worked in that they were always fighting each other but failed because they always had time to fight us too. We even tried to give some detainees more amenities if they listened to our commands. This made others in the same quad mad, and most of the time, they attacked the detainees who behaved. We didn't care though; it made them fight each other, and we had no problem with that.

We had to separate the Sunnis and the Shias because they would outright murder each other if given the chance. They were the biggest rival factions, so many times, we intermixed compounds by putting Shias in quads A and C and Sunnis in B and D. It made it more difficult for them to send messages to the other groups. In the other compounds, like the communals where everyone was housed together, people had to be the same religious affiliation.

Even within their own religious sects, there was a lot of violence. Overcrowding was in full force, which made for really angry detainees. The more extremist groups began to force other detainees to convert to a more radical form of Islam. Those who refused were beaten with bats, shocked with wiring, stabbed, burned, and many times, raped. The sexual assaults were so common that we had a term for it: "blood butt." Whenever the detainee could make it to the front of the quad, he would yell, "Sergeant, sergeant, blood butt," to get our attention. The term stuck. The detainees could do almost anything, including rape and murder, within their huts, and we had no way to stop them. We listened to the screams and got the medic ready for when they decided to quit.

Once the poor bastard agreed to convert or if his friends broke through the mob, he was brought to the front gate wrapped in a blanket. Thus, the term "blanket baby" was coined. Every time, we had the same conversation, no matter the compound. A few men would walk up with a blanket baby held between them. The man might still be groaning, crying, or silent. The guard would ask, "What happened?"

The detainees said, "Sergeant, Sergeant! He sick! He woke up like this!"

"Bullshit! He didn't wake up like this. Tell me what happened."

"Sergeant, it's true! He fell asleep and just woke up like this!"

"So you're telling me he went to sleep and woke up with burn marks on his nipples and broken legs?"

"Yes, Sergeant!"

"Wow, Allah must be really pissed at him!"

The same thing happened over and over; after a while, it just became routine.

These incidents didn't always happen because of extremist rhetoric; political posturing, gangs, and just general boredom were all reasons to harm each other. Some detainees of TSgt Holmes made feminine masks from paper and colored pencils. Then when the detainees ganged up on another one, they made him wear the mask while they raped him. Many times, detainees snuck up on each other at night and tried to kill each other just to gain more power politically. The first few dead bodies or injured detainees were a little shocking but very quickly ceased to surprise or bother me. When a hurt or dead detainee was brought up to the gate, we were given the irritating task of finding a medic to check on him. I didn't care if the detainee was dead or alive; I had more important things to do than waste my time looking for a doc.

For their actions, the detainees might get twenty-four hours in segregation; if they really pissed off the wrong people, other detainees would kill them. By the time most detainees reached Camp Bucca, they knew they wouldn't be leaving anytime soon. Many of them had been locked up for three or four years and hadn't even been to court once about their charges. They no longer cared about obeying any rules because it wouldn't help them, so they made up their own rules in quads and compounds and lived however they wanted.

To make matters more interesting, we also had ICOs and interpreters. ICOs were being trained in all parts of the TIF, QRF included. Supposedly, we were training them for when they eventually took control of the TIF. What a crock of shit! They never took control of the TIF, and a majority of the time, they were nothing but more people to look after and make sure they weren't trying to kill us too.

We had three separate groups that worked with QRF; each group worked five days and had ten days off. It was a beautiful schedule. Our first group of ICOs was awful. All they did was hide in our little air-conditioned building. They never went on digs or searches and absolutely never went on in- or out-processing. They wanted to go during riots so they could shoot the detainees, but we refused to let them hold any weapons. They were simply allowed to hold the shields; since none of us trusted them, we refused to let them be our shields. Once during a riot, when it got a little intense, they walked off. Their "sergeant" said it was their prayer and meal time, so they just left. After that, we rarely interacted with them; most of us just considered them detainees on parole and kept them close enough to still watch them.

Our second group was a bit better. They actually wanted to learn some of the work. A few of them thought they were better than digging around in the dirt, so they wouldn't do it. But this group was mostly made up of young single guys in their early twenties. They were looking for love by acquiring an American visa. I made the mistake of telling one of them that I was not married, and he followed me around for the rest of the day. Every time I started digging a hole, he came to finish it for me. Finally, he got a little creepy, so I told him that while I was unmarried, I already had several illegitimate children, each from a different man. The lie worked. He stayed away from me like I was the devil, and as an added bonus, he told all his young buddies, so they kept their distance too. This group also wanted the status of using weapons during riots, which our leadership denied. But they left the riots after getting hit with OC pepper spray or grenades. We kind of understood that—they didn't have any gas masks, only handkerchiefs, to use.

Our third group was amazing. They were in their late twenties to late thirties. Many of these men had lived through Saddam's regime, and they were ecstatic he was gone. Their "sergeant" was a guy I will call Ali; none of us knew their real names for safety reasons. He was a huge dude in his forties; he had been a boxer before we invaded. I asked him why he boxed into his forties as that was a long time. He simply said, "Saddam."

I was confused until he explained that Saddam's regime forced him to continue boxing or they would harm his family. He stopped at one point, and the regime killed one of his cousins in retaliation. Ali hated the whole former regime. This group would do whatever we were doing; they wanted to learn the job. I went through quite a few riots with them, and I personally had no problem with them as my shields. More importantly, they listened to a female holding their vest and directing them where to go. We did allow two or three guys in this group to actually use shotguns during a riot—Ali was one of them. He said it was an honor because he knew we didn't trust most of them with weapons.

I respected that almost all of them were putting their lives and their family's lives in jeopardy. If you worked with the Americans, the Iraqi resistance would find any way to get to you. If that meant killing you or any of your family, then so be it. Almost all the ICOs and interpreters covered their lower faces with handkerchiefs. Our QRF interpreter covered his mouth and jaw with a hankie. He wore a hat and sunglasses. And none of them ever used their real names, not even with each other, just in case one of them was a traitor or spy. Occasionally, a detainee came in, recognized an ICO, and yelled his name. After that, the ICO was "reassigned" overnight but probably left to take his family to safety. Either way, we never saw him again.

Casper was one of the very few ICOs who refused to cover his face; he was assigned to Ali's ICO group. When asked, he said he was not afraid of anyone, so he let them see his face. Casper was also secretly a Catholic. During Islamic prayer times, he either faked participation or hung out with us, depending on who was leading his group that day. One day, Casper was told that his father was very ill; he was given twenty days of leave to visit his family. We never saw him again. His father wasn't sick, but someone had found out he was working with us. They killed his whole family, and then when he arrived home, they killed him. At QRF, we only found out because Ali told us; he felt we needed to understand why he and most of his group were quitting. After that, our good group was gone. Not that any of us blamed them; the danger they faced on a daily basis was a total nightmare. They were replaced by a group that was completely resistant to any of our training. So we mostly ignored our ICOs from that point out.

We were always suspicious of our interpreter's allegiance. Riley seemed to appear right before any flight briefing and had a lot of questions for the leadership. On his days off, we found more contraband in the compounds we were searching than when he was with us. On days he accompanied us to compounds for searches or digs, we found a lot less contraband. He always loved to talk to us and questioned us about our families, homes, and anything American in general. This doesn't seem bad, but we had been trained to be suspicious of locals asking questions, especially about our families or where we lived. He might have just been curious, or maybe it was something more devious. We couldn't tell. Eventually, we reached the point where we specifically had someone make sure he stayed away from the intelligence briefings. In an old photo of my element, when we finally had a night off, Riley is in the middle of the group. We are all casually smiling and acting chill while knowing he was most likely a terrorist or spy. That's how fucked up we had to be, happy and enjoying the company of a terrorist.

By the end of our deployment, I tried not to deal with ICOs or interpreters at all. I didn't trust them, and at that point, I hated anyone who was Middle Eastern. Time and again, we found them breaking camp rules, like wandering into the American side of the base, supposedly accidentally. Riley was one of the chief culprits. At one point, we had to place guards around their camp to make sure none of them snuck away. Some were no better than the detainees; they were caught telling insurgents our base size, approximate personnel strength, detainee numbers, and all sorts of shit. Hell, at least one of them used a GPS tracker around the TIF. Some of them were probably all right, but I wasn't going to give any of them a chance. Many of us resented them because of the cultural work differences, which meant we did all the work and the ICOs mostly lazed around. I used to think, *Hey fucker, I'm in your country trying to help you, and you aren't doing anything but sitting on your ass. Get up and fix your own damn country!*

CHAPTER TEN

PUSHED AND STABBED

C ompound 18 was defying the guards in every way possible. They refused to line up for head counts, openly threw rocks at the tower guards while brazenly showing their faces, and once ripped through two fences to combine two quads. We were dispatched there almost daily. Every time we attempted to start a search or dig, they would riot.

Some of it probably had to do with the guards. Navy sailors took care of this compound and three others. No offense to the sailors at all, but they had absolutely no background in security or law enforcement. They went to Camp McGregor like we did; however, their training lasted a little bit longer. These sailors were mechanics, cooks, avionics, chefs and the like; after seven weeks, they were expected to know how to respond to serious threats. They did a great job for people with very little training; they adapted to the situations and did the best they could. They just needed additional help at times.

One reason I loved going to the Navy side for incidents was they just ran around with boxes of shotgun rounds. Any time we fired a round, Air-Fuck-You bureau-crazy required us to fill out a statement of how many rounds, what type, why, and what injuries the detainee sustained. We could never remember all that bullshit in the middle of a riot. But if I was on the Navy side, I could just take all my ammo out and put theirs in; once the riot ended, I replaced my rounds, and wham, bam, no report for me. I also made sure to keep a few extra rounds in case I might need them. Ah, the little things in life.

But Compound 18 was becoming a real problem; we got stuck out there for hours when they ripped the two quads open. All the detainees from one quad went into another quad, so instead of three hundred in each, we had six hundred in one. If it weren't so dangerous, it would have been hilarious. We were told to herd all the detainees from Quad A out of Quad D and back to their holding area while others repaired the fencing. I started laughing out loud. After a few minutes of trying to collect myself, I finally asked our Flight Sergeant how we were supposed to know who was assigned to Quad A. Detainees had an ID bracelet with a picture and their name but nothing else and definitely no quad assignments. TSgt V looked at me, smiled a little, and said, "I have no fucking clue."

For the next three hours, we stood around Quad D while Navy leadership tried to talk, compromise, and make deals to get the detainees back in the correct quads. The most disturbing sounds were coming from tents. We labeled one the love shack and the other the beating shack. The screams sounded almost the same at times, but one had a more animalistic desperation. We couldn't possibly drown out the noise, so we began to make bets on which detainee yelled the loudest, the most, etc. Making it a game gave it a somewhat surreal feeling, but it didn't soothe our screaming consciences. We missed our lunch while the leadership made them promises. Many of us (QRF and Navy) kept asking if we could just go full throttle and start crowd control with gas and randomly grab some and throw them in Quad A. We were told absolutely not; we needed to learn to compromise with them. My inside monster almost jumped out at that —almost, but not quite. *Compromise with them? The guys I'm watching rape one another like a haji porno on crack while also quite literally beating the shit out of one another for fun! Never, absolutely never!* I almost shot that reply back at my captain, but sanity slowly beat the monster down.

Eventually, the quad leaders agreed to separate, and Quad A went back to their area. At least, we hoped so. Once they realized they had forced the Americans to compromise, shit just went downhill from there. We started responding to Compound 18 daily, in addition to all our other jobs. The compound detainees began telling their guards that they would kill any American that entered their area and make a big show of it. They even dug shallow graves in the middle of their common area and told the Navy person in charge that they wanted to kill an American in the grave and make everyone watch them die. Just lovely.

Finally, we were told that we had to do a search of Compound 18. *It's about time*! We knew it wouldn't be easy; they would fight us every step of the way. We arrived at the compound with all our tools plus riot gear, and as an added measure, our Flight Sergeant had some of us bring along our M4s and M9s. They were secured in a vehicle just in case.

The Navy person in charge of the compound went to speak with the quad chief in Quad D. They were our first search area for the day. The chief began yelling at him and at the detainees in Arabic. Most of the detainees began to gather in their middle area just out of reach of our shotguns while a few stayed in their tents.

We began to tense up, waiting for the first shouts of "Allah Ackbar" and rocks to come raining down. It never happened. Instead, a few of the men grabbed another detainee, dragged him down to the small grave they had made for us, and stabbed him in the stomach twice. Then they left him there. We couldn't go in after him; they refused to go to their holding area. For almost an hour, we stood in the heat with full gear on, watching this man slowly die. Apparently, this detainee was a snitch, and for some reason, they thought we would move into the quad to save him. We didn't—we waited and waited for him to die. Hearing rapes and beatings and now watching someone slowly die cemented the thought that detainees were nothing but violent animals, stupid beasts that needed a bigger, meaner animal to crush them. One thought kept running through my mind. *Dammit, I'm missing lunch again!* I had moved past the point of viewing them as people; hell, they didn't care about killing each other, why should we care? He was just one less head to count during shift; none of us would be shedding any tears at his death.

Their message was entirely clear though; they wanted to kill us and were begging for a fight. So were we—the idea of taking Compound 18 down was fast becoming an obsession. The TIF commander couldn't overlook or compromise the act of an open murder; they had forced him to take action.

On a cold, rainy March morning somewhere around 0800 hours, we gathered in the open field near Compound 18. This field area would become QRF's new home in about a month, but at that time, it held nothing but sand. We began preparing for conducting a hard push, something that had been explained to us in training but we had never seen, let alone done. We had no way to practice it without the detainees seeing us, so we had to do one with only a blackboard drawing as an explanation.

The concept is quite easy and is broken down into three groups: Group A, the initial team of about ten, entering the quad; Group B, a second team of about twenty-six, staggered with batons and shields; and Group C, the last team of at least seventy-five people. Group A stacks up close to the gates where two non-lethal claymore mines are detonated. The team opens the gate immediately afterward and enters the quad. They begin in the farthest huts from the holding area and throw a stinger grenade into the hut. After it detonates, they enter the hut, clearing it. They do this at each hut, pushing any detainees toward the middle area and down toward the holding area. As Group A does this, Group B enters the area in the same spot as Group A. Their job is to hold a straight line from the nearest hut to the fence.

They must hold that area to allow Group C to enter the quad. Group C rushes through the fence gate and forms at the middle area between the huts farthest from the holding area. They then march down the middle area, catching all the detainees still fighting and the ones that Group A throws out of the huts. Once they reach the holding area gates, both Groups A and C begin physically pushing detainees into the holding area. Group B conducts another sweep through the huts to make sure no one is left and provides additional reinforcement, pushing anyone left into the holding area.

The first issue was the personnel for all of QRF and both shifts, along with teams of ten-, twenty-six-, and seventy-five-man teams, were maybe seventy people. The math didn't quite work. So we improvised. The TIF commander had any and all extra personnel from all compounds report to the field. He had the K-9 handlers with their dogs come too; they were attached to the initial entry teams clearing out the huts. So now, the entire TIF was waiting on what we would do in Compound 18; since all the extra people were with us, no one was available for shift change or anything else. So no one got to leave the TIF until 18 was dealt with. That day, almost every TIF guard worked sixteen–eighteen hours, regardless of their shift.

The whole huge mass of us assembled in that field, which was quickly becoming a muddy pit. We loosely organized ourselves, according to which group we were in: I was in Group B, SSgt Orleans was in Group A, Taylor was one of the unlucky suckers who had to stay in her compound, and TSgt Holmes had the best spot of all—she was in the tower of the Air Force compound right across from 18.

At the gates of Quad D, the detainees were throwing their usual fun items at us: man-gurt, rocks, concrete, feces, and urine. They even seemed a little surprised by the large number of people. The TIF commander was even there; he gave the quad chief one more order to go to the holding area in hopes they would all listen. The chief complied, but almost no one else did. Two people set up the mines; we tightened up, got our last breaths of clean air, and pulled on our gas masks. The tower guards in each corner of the quad threw gas grenades inside, and the claymore mines were triggered.

One mine blasted off; the other was a dud. In Group A went, running into the smoky haze with dogs barking. Group B ran right behind them; the airman in front of me tripped slightly, and suddenly, I tripped too. I looked down; we were all tripping and kicking the dud claymore. I barely had time to think. *Thank God, it's a dud. Bam*! It wasn't a dud, just a delayed explosion. It blew up right as Group C was heading into the quad; suddenly, we were down about eight people in that group. Detainees were running pell-mell to the holding area, being chased by dog handlers; they were terrified of the dogs. *What the hell? Is that dog walking two-legged, or is he melted into a detainee's chest?* But as soon as I blinked, it was gone. Detainees couldn't get into the holding area fast enough. It was so satisfying, seeing these assholes who had been threatening us, now screaming and running in terror.

Once Quad D was fully into the holding area, we moved on to Quad A, the other breakout quad. The TIF commander gave their chief the order to go to the holding area. The chief started with a little attitude and trying to compromise again; the commander called for us to line up in formation. As soon as the claymore mines (which I was a little afraid of now) were placed at their gates, the chief switched approaches and began to scream at the detainees to move. They went with a little piss and attitude, a few rocks and crap thrown, but they went into the holding cell. When the TIF commander went to Quads B and C, they were already in their holding areas.

After all detainees were where they needed to be, we headed back to the open field for our debriefing. While we were out there, we had some smoke-and-joke time; some of us hadn't really seen each other since arriving at Bucca, so we laughed and caught up. Our squadron commander was there as well, walking around and talking. I ran into SSgt Orleans, and she described a moment during the hard push when one of the K-9s almost bit her. She said she panicked and grabbed a detainee and threw him in front of her. The dog latched onto his chest, and the detainee ran away screaming. So what I saw wasn't an illusion—a dog really was attached to a detainee's chest. After about an hour, we all began to disperse, most of us heading to various compounds to start our shifts.

I got over to QRF, and we did our shift change to start our fourteen-hour shift. Our Flight Sergeant had told the other Shift Sergeant not to come in until 0200 instead of 2400. The other shift had worked from 2400 until 1400, so it was only fair. To help us that night, TSgt V bought pizzas and coffee from Pizza Hut and Green Beans for the whole flight. It was still cold and rainy; we were totally nasty from mud, rain, sweat, OC gas, and detainee stench. I've never had a better feast than that slightly soggy, lukewarm pizza and coffee cooled past the yum phase. That was the last time we ever had major problems from Compound 18. We were sent out there occasionally for fights plus we still did random searches and digs, but we never had more issues with outright rebellion. But when we did go there, tangible hatred oozed from them. They didn't say anything, but we saw it in their eyes, the way they walked, and even in their shortened breathing.

Right around this time, we got our first call to help with an injury to a service member. We loaded up in the trucks and then were told to unload and grab all our search-and-dig equipment in addition to our riot gear. After we grabbed everything, we headed over to the Navy side compounds. On our way there, we kept trying to figure out what we were going to be doing because all we knew was someone got hurt. That's it: not how, why, or who.

Our first sign that something was up was that the whole compound—Quads A–D—was silent. No detainees were walking around, no normal chatting, nothing. One detainee stuck his head out of his hut, and the tower guard blasted him with the shotgun with no warning. "What the hell happened?" The whispers floated up and down our lines. Whatever it was, the Navy guys had pulled out all the stops and were suddenly not the easy-going sailors we had been working with.

We gathered around TSgt V, and he told us what had happened. That night during head count, a detainee had stabbed one of the sailors in the neck with a toothbrush. The detainees' bracelets had a picture on it, so guards were required to match the picture with the detainee's face. There was really no safe way to do this; the most secure way was to lift up the detainee's arm to check the picture but still control the hand. But really, if he wanted to stab you, he could. Thankfully, the toothbrush wasn't too sharp and only went in a little way. Also, the sailor had the presence of mind to grab the detainee's arm and bring it down on the metal crossbeam of the check area, thus shattering the guy's forearm.

He had been rushed to the TIF hospital, more out of fear of infection than depth of the stab; sometimes, they would soak their weapons in urine or feces. The Navy wanted us to help get the guy who hurt their sailor. Somehow, in all the commotion, he slipped away from the gate and into a hut. In addition, after we got him, their shift leader wanted us to search the whole area and every detainee. "Tear every fucking unauthorized thing to shreds" were his exact words. These Navy guys were pissed. Not that I blamed them, I would have been blackout angry if one of my team members got hurt too.

First, TSgt V tried to convince the quad chief to bring the guy up. He kept telling the chief, "Your man is injured and needs medical attention. Let us treat him." The quad chief didn't believe a word of it; he knew his guy was in big shit. Next, TSgt V told him to line up his people; they needed to head into the holding area while we searched the area. The quad chief said no to that too. So TSgt V pulled out the big guns; he gave the quad chief one last directive to line up his people, or we would come in there like we did at Compound 18. The quad chief caved at that threat.

So as the detainees began lining up and heading into the holding area, we kept an eye out for someone with a messed-up arm. With more than three hundred people milling around, he managed to slip into the holding area. No matter, though, we would be pulling them out by groups of ten and searching them after we finished searching the quad. Let him suffer with a smashed-up arm. Just like the Navy compound leader wanted, we tore up that place.

It was now the beginning of the hot season, so they didn't need their coats anymore. We took them. If it looked like a detainee had too many pants or shirts, we took those as well. And we took every single toothbrush that we found too. We found more shanks, chai rocks, messages in Arabic from different compounds, unused FN 303 rounds, Iraqi money, and all sorts of shit.

After we finished searching their living area, we began bringing them out ten at a time into the walkway. There, they were searched and resecured in the living area. The quad leader didn't like this because he knew we were hunting for the offending detainee; he started to yell and threaten the Navy leader. The Navy leader told him to either do the search or sit in the holding area for the rest of his deployment but, either way, to shut the fuck up. I started laughing at that point; these Navy guys were cool when they were pissed. The quad leader finally gave up; he brought up the assailant and turned him over to the Navy leader. Our team quickly searched him, and then, a couple of our guys took him to the TIF hospital to check out his mangled arm. Even the Navy leader didn't trust that some accident wouldn't happen if he sent his own sailors. Again, if it were my team, I know there would have been an accident.

After we got all that sorted out, the Navy leader told the quad chief that because he didn't obey the commands, we were still going to search all the detainees. The quad leader was being put in one of their twelve-hour isolation boxes. So we searched him and moved him to the isolation box. After that, we had no problems with other detainees talking back or trying to bargain with any of us. We finished up, dropped off all the contraband we found, and headed back to the QRF shack after what was altogether a productive day.

CHAPTER ELEVEN

CRACKED DREAMS

*I might kill someone today. I might die today. Eh, who cares. We all
die at some point.* I was beginning to realize that life could easily
be taken away, but that didn't seem to concern me anymore. I wasn't
going out and trying to get hurt or doing anything rash, but watching
detainees get hurt or die didn't bother me at all. Seeing an injured or
dead detainee was quickly becoming a daily event; in my head, if it
was one of them and not one of us, that's all that mattered. They
would fling piss, poop, man-gurt, and other specimens at us daily.
Who does that? So they were less than human to me and, therefore,
not worthy of my pity or concern.

I kept having the same disturbing dream every night. It started out
simply enough; I was at home visiting my family. We were all
gathered around the dinner table, just conversing and having a great
time. One by one, each of my family members began to attack me,
first verbally, then physically; so I ran around the house, outside, or
wherever I could to get away. Night after night, this repeated dream
became worse until, eventually, they were trying to kill me.

One night, instead of trying to run away, I fought back. The dream began to do a slow reverse so that instead of running, I was gradually fighting more and more until I was killing my whole family. Almost every night for the rest of my deployment, I had some variation of the same dream. I started sleeping less and less because I was afraid to sleep. I actually worried I was going a little crazy because each night, it was easier and easier to kill them. I began to be a little afraid of going home. It affected me deeply—it has been fifteen years since my deployment, and I still remember every progression of the dream sequence to this day.

"This will be the last time you hear about another extension!" Col. Shell bellowed. We were all standing outside in the April heat, receiving our second official extension and the November crew's third one. We were now scheduled to leave in late August, and they were supposedly leaving in June. By the drooped shoulders and vacant stares, Col. Shell knew we didn't believe him. It wasn't his fault that we were being extended; there was nothing he could do. The Surge was in full effect, and extensions were the norm for many units in Iraq.

In the middle of the formation, SSgt Bird stepped to the back, began sobbing, and repeating, "My marriage is over! My wife said she'll leave if I get extended again." A chaplain and higher-ranking NCO escorted him toward the chapel. Col. Shell continued his speech about how we would continue to do a great job on the mission and blah, blah, blah. I tuned him out.

Bird wouldn't be the last person to have a breakdown; I felt really bad for the people who were married, dating, or parents. The separation inflicts chaos on the heart and especially the mind. It was easy to be in Iraq and think your spouse was cheating—you would never know. I had never deployed while married or dating, so it was no big deal to me. Not that being extended was okay; I just couldn't relate to the married or parental aspect. Many people were divorced or in the middle of divorcing by the time we left Bucca. Deployments are incredibly stressful not only for the military member but for their spouses and families as well. Intermittent contact and extensions make it easy for those at home to think about what their loved one might be doing. And well, the longer the deployment stretched on, people did cheat both here and at home. The longer the deployment lasted, the more home felt unreal. The only thing that seemed real was Bucca and what was happening in that moment.

During that Commander's Call, I realized that we wouldn't be leaving anytime soon. I figured if I just stopped thinking it would ever happen, it might be easier to keep a clear head. "I will never leave here. This is where I'll live the rest of my life" became my new mantra. I used it to numb any warm feelings about the idea of going home.

People talk about going home almost as soon as deployment begins. First, it's excitedly discussed as leaving home on an adventure and then coming back again. As the deployment lengthens, the topic becomes more wistful. Near the end, it's all about what you will do when you get home, who you will see first, what you will eat, how drunk you will get. Home is in nearly every conversation in one way or another. By training my mind not to think about home, I was severing that connection to sanity and, most importantly, to my humanity. I was opening the door of my psyche and letting my monster out to wreak havoc.

I still called my parents and friends but less than before. When I was on the phone, I couldn't connect with them like I used to. It was hard to talk about how my day was when I knew telling them would only make them worry more. Plus, what could I really say? "Today, I saw a detainee crap in a bag and throw it at us, and another one got caught doing something bad, so they took him into a tent and beat him. How was your day?" I've learned those kinds of details scare most people. In a way, the disconnect was helpful; it slightly lessened the power of that awful dream as I convinced myself I would stay in Bucca forever. I figured it was all right to feel less guilty about that dream because I would probably never see my family again.

CHAPTER TWELVE

FUN TIMES AT COMPOUND 2

B y April, the heat was beginning to hit in full force, yet the detainees continued to riot almost daily. Now they had been coordinating among themselves so that most riots were in multiple compounds at once, usually in Compounds 4, 10, and 16. Compound 4 was another overflow for the segregation unit because Compound 6 was now overflowing into 4. Compound 10, where Taylor worked, had recently received more radicalized detainees from Camp Cropper, and they were making power plays. Compound 16 was overflowing with absolute assholes. The other compounds still rioted from time to time, but these were our regulars.

Then we began to hear of problems in Compound 2, which was one of the few communals with over a thousand detainees housed in one big open space. Communals were incredibly hard to stop a riot in because they had a big open area that our shotguns and FN 303s couldn't reach. So if a communal rioted, we only had to get as close to the fence as possible and wait it out. We had done that at Compound 7 when they rioted, and it seemed to work all right.

But when the chemist arrived at Camp Bucca, he was placed in

Compound 2. He was obviously well-educated and connected within the unofficial terrorist hierarchy, and he was about to make our lives even more miserable.

One day, while hanging around the QRF compound, a riot began at Compound 2. Depending on how far away you are, what you hear first will vary. Normally, it starts as a very uneasy quiet within the compound. Almost everyone is in their huts or tents, and it's just creepy quiet. This sets the tower guards and rovers on edge. Then detainees begin clustering outside their huts with their faces wrapped up and wearing long pants and their heavy winter jackets. Now it's normally over 100 degrees every day, so the winter jacket is a dead giveaway. Next, one or two detainees will begin their chant, always something in Arabic. The now-gathered mass will scream back, "Allah Ackbar." Then it's officially game on: rocks, concrete, poop, man-gurt, urine, and more start flying in all directions as the tower guards begin to shoot in response.

When Compound 2 started rioting, we barely heard the chant because of distance, but then the shotguns fired off. Still, we had to wait until their compound leader officially called us, so we just got on our gear and weapons, loaded up in the trucks, and waited. A couple of guys had radios that monitored the TIF; most of ours were set to the QRF channel. Over the static on one radio, the compound leader called, "QRF requesting backup." With whoops and hollers, we started the trucks and headed down the Green Mile. One of our guys had a portable iPod with speakers, and for many of our riots, we would ride in listening to "Riot" by Three Days Grace as our motivation song.

Once we got to Compound 2, we were briefed to hold fire because of the size of it unless we were absolutely sure we could hit the detainees. Otherwise, we were staggered with two shields and one shotgun and told to get as close as possible to the fence. Basically, all we could do was watch them riot and keep them away from the fence so, hopefully, they couldn't break free. That day, my two shield guys—Tom Richardson and Tom Bryan (this is why the military uses only last names)—were both from my home base, so we knew each other really well. They were great guys who were both an easy 6'3" each while I'm 5'5". While they held shields, nothing would hit me in the face. But there was one small problem. With their height, holding the shield correctly opened my entire lower half from the hips down to hits. Once we fought our way to the fence, I would be fine, but until we reached it, I was pelted quite a few times right in the shins. Ouch!

After about an hour, the detainees unveiled their newest weapon: the fiery oranges. At first, they were kind of neat to watch; they would fly through the air and hit the fence with sparks shooting everywhere. It was kind of pretty. But once they hit something, they didn't bounce nor did the flames go out. They were coated with something so that the orange would stick to an object and continue to burn. Suddenly, the oranges were not so fun. Others reported that some of the rocks being flung at them had nails and screws sticking out. One particularly large rock cracked one of our shields.

Eventually, the detainees tired themselves out and calmed down. After the debacle of Compound 18, no compound leader would even think of compromising with the detainee chiefs, so until they were all done, we watched while they burned shit and threw stuff at us. It got boring after a while. But we finished the riot and went back to our area to wait for the next fun event.

About two days later, the announcement came. "QRF, respond to Compound 2 immediately!" The call went out on all our radios, and our previously quiet afternoon suddenly erupted into a frenzy of activity. By now, we had perfected our pre-riot gear routine; at the beginning of every shift, each person signed out their respective shield, baton, mace, and shotgun and had them placed in rows on the trucks with our helmets and flak vest. Each helmet had our name written on the front and back, so every person knew exactly where to

go and which gear to put on. The only exception was the shotguns—
these were either carried or placed in our mobile armory, which went
with us to riots.

That day, we had just finished an in-processing and were
recuperating for a bit when suddenly that yell came over the radio,
not on the TIF station but on the direct QRF line so every one of our
radios picked it up. In less than a minute, we were all on the trucks,
and they were driving toward Compound 2. We were so rushed, we
forgot our motivational riot song, but as we arrived, not much seemed
to be happening. There was some yelling but not toward the front,
and it was small for a communal of over a thousand people. But the
tower guards on the left side seemed pretty agitated by something on
that side of the compound. They kept shooting shotgun rounds, but
the detainees were out of range. A team of us grabbed our weapons
and jumped off the trucks headed in that direction. Our REV 113
drove in front of us, and we used it as cover from the rocks and crap
flying around us. As we turned the corner, the problem was clear: a
detainee was near the top of the fence! I started chuckling, thinking
this had to be the stupidest idiot to try to climb the fence in full view
of two towers! But as we got close to him, he didn't seem to be trying
to escape as much as trying to not fall back into the crowd
underneath him. The mob was actually throwing rocks and hitting
him with tent poles. When he saw us, he began screaming, "They kill
me!" over and over.

He had been mistakenly placed in the wrong compound and was
a different religious affiliation than Compound 2, and they were
indeed trying to kill him. So as a last-ditch effort, he climbed the
fence to get away from the lynch mob and to get the compound's
attention. We never found out how this mistake happened, not that it
mattered to me anyhow.

We went to work, shooting detainees away from the fence, trying
to get them back so he could get down. We told him to climb down

inside the compound, and we would personally escort him to the front and to safety. He refused to drop down inside the compound as he was simply too terrified and did not believe that he would be safe. He had gotten slightly stuck at the top of the fencing in rings of C-wire and razor wire, unforgiving sharp strands that can actually cut right into your femoral artery if you aren't careful. So now, we had to somehow safely extract him from the fence and keep the others from attacking him and us.

TSgt V decided to use the REV 113 as the base for a short ladder. He placed the ladder on top of the 113 and propped it against the fence. Next, he used a detainee mattress to throw over parts of the wires, and up he climbed. He reached the detainee and helped him untangle, and they slid safely down the ladder. Once the detainee got to the ground, he turned to say thank you and actually dropped to his knees. We secured him with shackles and handcuffs and led him off. We probably didn't need to cuff him since he was a complete mess; the other detainees had gotten to him before he reached the fence and worked him over pretty well. Because we thought he was escaping, he was hit with shotgun rounds a few times and rocks and crap from the detainees. On top of all that, he was pretty cut up from the C-wire and razor wire; basically, he could barely stand, let alone run away.

Once we had secured him, the riot began in earnest. They were pissed that we had pulled him from their grasp. They lit caravans on fire, slingshot rocks, and fire oranges like crazy. The rocks actually broke a few of the bulletproof windows in the tower guard. Our captain was present and ordered us not to fire back unless we could get the detainee who was flinging objects. In order to do that, you had to open yourself up to getting hit by exposing at least some of your body around your shield. My shield and I were so frustrated by that order that we just stood near the fence, unable to shoot.

At one point, a detainee flung a fire orange that sailed too high over the fence to hit us. I screamed out, "Ha! Stupid motherfucker, you missed!" So much stuff came pouring down around us in the space of thirty seconds: shitbags, man-gurt, rocks, little rocks, and more.

After the barrage stopped and we could breathe without the danger of poop in the nose, A1C Hernandez, my shield holder, turned to me and said, "O'Brien, please never do that to me again."

I coughed a bit. "Yeah, that was my bad. I didn't think they would do that."

The look in her eyes said, "I will kill you if you make that shit happen again!"

The fire oranges not only melted things but could actually start objects on fire. All the towers in the TIF were metal, but they all had different types of camo netting draped over them to help create some shade during the day. Woosh! Those camo nets went up like dried-out paper. The tower guards kept their heads and successfully put out the fires before anything was burned too badly. They then got permission to use the gas grenades. The shotguns were not effective because they were too short range. Suddenly, we were choking on gas. Our radios were on a different frequency than the tower guards, so we didn't hear the clearance given for gas. We did have gas masks that worked well; I used mine more times than I can count. However, if you get hit with gas and then place the gas mask on, it effectively seals the gas in with you. I have done this before as well. So once we were hit with the gas, all we could do was power through it. I fell back on what worked in the OC training: anger. As the detainees were choking and coughing from the gas, I started laughing at them and telling them that I was an evil, infidel American woman, and the gas didn't bother me. I continued telling them that they were weaker than an unholy woman and didn't deserve to be called men. At this point, I might have gone off the deep end, but thankfully, before anything else could happen, A1C Hernandez grabbed me and said we had been called back. The riot was officially over.

CHAPTER THIRTEEN

PROMOTED WITH EXPLOSIONS

O n May 1, I officially promoted to Staff Sergeant. A new NCO promotion is a significant jump in all military branches; it signifies that you are no longer in the low enlisted bracket and you are now responsible for training and supervising others. And the really big perk is a generous pay raise. The promotion ceremony is generally a little more serious than for E-4 and below as well.

When a person promotes, they are allowed to pick two higher-ranking people to tag on their stripes. They each take a side, punch the ever-loving crap out of the area where your new stripe is, switch sides, and hit you again. Once you get back to your duty section, you will run the gauntlet. You then walk down the line and get pounded by everyone who is your new rank and above, then turn around and come back. I'm not certain why, but at Bucca, we had added to the gauntlet tradition by allowing everybody, no matter their rank, to punch the new sergeant. We walked the first part and then ran after the turnaround. It's totally about morale boosting and a weird way to celebrate someone's achievement.

On the day of my promotion, I was given the day off to make sure

I had a new—or should I say, up-to-date—uniform. If I went to work, there was always the chance that I might not make it back in time for the promotion ceremony. Our ceremony wasn't until around 2000 hours, so I had almost the whole day off. The ceremony was so late because we had now officially hit Iraqi summertime; daytime temperatures easily soared into triple digits and got a little hotter day by day.

That day, while waiting for the ceremony, I re-ironed my uniform at least twice and took an extra-long shower. I also got a fresh haircut and then went and took another quick shower to get rid of the little hairs. I went to dinner, and I think I went to call my parents. When I returned to my pod, I flipped on the lights and—surprise! Taylor, who wasn't able to come to the promotion ceremony because of her schedule, and my roommate Rahn had decorated my entire half of the room. They had yellow tape with Caution: New SSgt taped to it and SSgt paper stripes hanging from strings all over the room. My helmet was sporting large paper SSgt stripes as well. It was an incredible gesture, especially in that environment. I still have some of the pictures, including one they took while decorating. They were taking selfies before that was even a thing.

That evening, I dressed in my new uniform and headed down to the squadron and platform area. On my way down, multiple people kept stopping me and saying, "Congratulations." I didn't even know most of them: some were from the AF, the Army, and even a couple from the Navy. Apparently, an email had gone out to the base server with the names of all those who were promoted. I was completely surprised since I never checked my email. It was very nice, especially in an area with so many challenges; each positive moment made a lasting impact.

Once at the platform area, I went into the squadron and found Rahn. I hugged her and thanked her for the decorations. She made me take a few pictures in the squadron, and then we headed outside to get ready for formation. Four or five others were promoting that night as well. We formed up, and the ceremony began.

Col. Shell was officiating, and he spoke a few words about the responsibility that comes with becoming an NCO. Honestly, I don't remember too much of it because my nerves were starting to get the best of me. We began to swear in as NCOs, raising our right hand and repeating after Chief Mack. Then, one by one, we went up to receive our certificates and take a picture with the Chief and Lt. Col.

I don't know why, but I always had a secret fear that I would salute with the wrong hand. Someone actually did this once when I was a young airman, and the fear has never left me. Thankfully, I saluted correctly, received my certificate, smiled, and moved on. Now for the fun part, the tagging on.

I had asked TSgt Holmes and TSgt Moore, who was from Little Rock, to tag my stripes on. I admired both of them as leaders and NCOs. TSgt Moore had been my flight chief at Little Rock, and he regularly challenged me to think and act like an NCO who leads by example, not just force. TSgt Holmes was one of the first female NCOs in authority that I had met; she made sure that at every point of our training, she participated although the senior enlisted officers were not required to do so. Both of these individuals fulfilled what I felt was the most important portion of the Non-Commissioned Officer's Creed: "I will strive to know my people and use their skills to the maximum degree possible. I will always place their needs above my own and will communicate with my supervisor and my people and never leave them uninformed."

I'm not sure how many other people went before I had to go back up for my tagging. While I was up there, TSgt Holmes on my right and TSgt Moore on my left were chuckling evilly. They counted to three and *bam!* TSgt Moore's hit slammed me right into TSgt Holmes's on-coming punch. They ping-ponged me, so I stayed upright. Then they switched and did it again. Thankfully, the entire saluting of officers was done because all I could feel was some tingling in each arm.

Afterward, I went with TSgt Holmes and SrA Boyd to midnight chow. Once we finished eating, we headed to the pods to hang out for a bit. Well, the asshole insurgents had other plans. While walking, a *boom, boom, boom* echoed in the distance. I flinched a bit, Boyd hit the ground, and TSgt Holmes just kept walking. After a few feet, she turned around and said, "Hey, standing around won't make them stop."

Laughing, we all started walking again until the incoming sirens started up. We found a dug-out shelter and waited it out. Then we headed over to accountability, which was done rather quickly that night; by now, we had the whole routine down cold. It was a little bit of a damper on a fun evening, but that's Bucca; she's a bitch who will always steal your happiness.

I had forgotten about the whole flight gauntlet until the next day at guard mount. TSgt V broke us up into two lines two feet apart, making about a four-foot walking path. For a second, I actually wondered who had promoted that we were going to tag. He called me to the front of the rows and asked me if I wanted the Senior Airman and below to step out of the formation. Internally, hell, yes, I wanted that, but I never admitted it. I told them, "No, go right ahead." The first portion wasn't too bad; most of the huge muscled guys weren't going to pound a female, so I wasn't too afraid of them.

Then I turned around and started running. I was smacked from my shoulders down to my hips; once you start running, everyone has to hit faster, and their aim is sometimes off. Right after that, SSgt Orleans, or as I would now call her, Eliza, came up to me and said, "Wait, I missed the last arm," and *whap*! hit my arm again. Then we all loaded up in the trucks, and off to work we went.

The first stop of the day was Compound 2, where I was sure a riot would happen. More than thirteen hundred restless detainees had been crowded into their small holding area for almost sixteen hours. By this point, everyone was seasoned enough to sense when the detainees were ready to explode. A certain electricity zips through the air, kind of like the feeling you get when a tornado is about to touch down. It's going to happen; you just don't know when.

We had arrived at work and found our off-going shift at Compound 2 doing a full search with full body searches at the end. They told us, "Listen up! Compound 2 has lost three stinger grenades. Off-going has been searching the living area since they got on shift at midnight last night. So far, none of the grenades have been found. You guys will continue to search every damn tent, hut, and person until we find them. Nothing is out of bounds. Tear the huts down from roof to floor if you have to."

Everyone started swearing quietly. If our other shift had been in the living area for twelve hours and hadn't found anything, then the logical conclusion was that the detainees had smuggled the grenades into the holding area. This meant that whenever we finished tearing their living area apart, we would have to search every single person before they were allowed back in. All thirteen hundred of them. That alone would probably take close to eight hours.

The other shift members were filthy and exhausted but had found some interesting items: two tunnels, around fifty pounds of chai rocks, hundreds of beat sticks, and even some old food squirreled away. Detainees would save bread, water, oranges, and milk for riots, so if we tried to withhold food to get them to stop, they wouldn't have to succumb to a hunger strike. As for meat at their meals, huge rats were always around, and some detainees killed birds with slingshots and ate them.

The off-going shift was clearly happy to be leaving. From the stares and angry hisses from the detainees in the holding area, the riot would be starting any minute. One off-going guy said, "Good luck, guys, those fuckers are pissed and ready to explode. I hope they start before you search all of them. Also, we never got to search the WC. Enjoy!"

We thanked him with a multitude of "fuck you" and "I hope you fall off the five-ton." It was my lucky day to search the WC, so I wrapped up my face in a scarf and headed in. I made it all of thirty or forty seconds before I had to sprint back out to open air and vomit. The inside of the WC is concrete with no lights. During the day, it's almost pitch black; it was one of the few places where I was always a little nervous that a detainee might hide. After two more puke breaks, I decided it was clear enough, and if they had hidden the grenades in the shitholes, then they would never work anyhow. Our group moved on to the outside of the WC area. It was a permanently muddy little patch of ground; digging there always turned up some interesting surprises. Today was no exception—we found multiple shanks and piles of shit; some were even combined shank-shit piles like a disgusting little present.

We moved on from the WC area and continued digging and searching the living area for about four more hours. TSgt V was true to his word; we were tearing apart the huts, ripping through walls, and destroying the detainees' little homemade attics. Everywhere we searched, we found stuff: shanks, beat sticks, chai rocks, another tunnel, and even pieces of fence post flattened and sharpened into swords. Compound 2 was apparently ready to do some serious shit. Still, after more than sixteen hours of combined searching and seventeen hours of lockdown in their very small holding area, we found no grenades. Body search time had finally arrived.

TSgt V managed to get a few more guys to assist us, so instead of searching ten detainees at a time, we could search fifteen. Normally, when we were finished with a compound search, we would only search a percentage—10, 20, or 25 percent—of detainees. Because we were looking for something specific that any detainee could be hiding, we had to search every single person. Everyone knew they would riot rather than let us find the grenades or the detainees who had them. When searching detainees, one person does the actual body search, and an overwatch searches the extra items, like books, clothes, etc. Only men were allowed to search the detainees because of their religious and cultural differences. I had no complaints about that; I didn't want to touch the nasty fuckers anyways. During the body searches, the guys would occasionally get a surprise. We found at least one hermaphrodite and quite a number of detainees were turned on by the search. It was always hilarious to watch the airman's expression when he noticed how happy the detainee was. More than once, we had to pull a guy away from attacking the detainee.

We began with the first round of fifteen detainees. They were marched into a gated area adjacent to the holding area. Because Compound 2 was a communal, the holding area was larger than most quads, but it also had a secondary fenced area for overflow. We were using that secondary area as our search area, and we had stationed the REV 113 along the fence, dividing the full holding area and our secondary one. The first group was pretty disgruntled but mostly silent and compliant. We released them into the living area and grabbed the next group. The first group immediately disappeared into their huts and began talking angrily with each other. The second group finished and was put into the living area; we started searching group three. This group was argumentative and refusing our commands. My gut tightened; the riot would be starting soon. TSgt V had us grab our riot gear after group three was put in the living area. As I came back from getting my gear and shotgun, some of the detainees in the living areas were now back outside the huts. They had wrapped up their faces (a definite riot sign), and many held slingshots, beat sticks, and mini swords. We had just searched each of them and that living area for over sixteen hours, and we still didn't find all their contraband. It was incredibly frustrating.

As we began searching group 4, detainees in the living and

holding areas began slowly chanting. *Thank God, they are going to start this before we search most of them*, I thought. *Now we won't be dog tired and stuck in a riot.* Suddenly it started: a shout in Arabic came from one of the detainees being searched. He was pointing to his Quran lying on the ground. He had probably thrown it there and tried to blame the airman searching him. This was typical—their Qurans were off limits to us; only the ICOs could touch them. The detainees commonly placed Qurans in areas where we might knock them to the ground or touch them. Once, I was clearing a hut, and they had placed a large bucket of water next to their box of Qurans. I could either fall in the water or trip over the Qurans. Somehow, I managed to do something even more unspeakable: I tripped and kicked the water bucket over the box of Qurans. The immediate riot lasted almost the entire shift. I felt bad because our team was stuck in the heat, but I kept laughing every time I remembered the looks on those detainees' faces when their Qurans were tipped out of the tent by waves of water. It was priceless.

The Quran drop was the signal for the riot; detainees in holding began ripping the fence links and running into their living area. We grabbed the fifteen detainees we had been searching and threw them back into the holding area; the rest of us fell into our shield-gunner formation and pushed against the fence separating our area from the living area. Detainees had immediately begun forming into well-organized groups with slingshots and mattresses for protection; they were slowly advancing toward our fence while we desperately shot round after round. It was useless though. The numbers were thirteen hundred to forty; there weren't enough rubber bullets to stop them. TSgt V yelled that we were going to back up slowly and use the REV for cover while trying to leave.

There was one tiny problem; the REV wouldn't start. The driver tried repeatedly, but it was completely dead. Out of the corner of my right eye, a stinger grenade flew toward our group. It hit the shield of the person next to me and bounced back about ten feet before exploding. Little black rubber balls flew everywhere, hitting SrA Meade (who was holding my shield) and me all along the right side of our bodies. It wasn't nice but didn't hurt too bad; the grenade had been pretty far from us but not so for the guys whose shield it hit. They weren't seriously injured, but a few of the balls embedded in their arms.

But where did the grenade come from? The closest tower to us was at such an angle that the guard would have needed to pivot away from the living area and throw in almost the opposite direction, so it couldn't have been from him. One guy to the left of me yelled, "That fucker has a grenade," right as the second grenade came flying over the fence. TSgt V did say we were staying until we got all three grenades back. We had two so far; now we only needed one more.

By now, we were almost shooting at point-blank range; the detainees were incredibly close, and some were even trying to stick their fence posts through the chain link. Every round we shot hit detainees, mostly in their faces. Some of the beads embedded while others peeled the skin off in strips. But there were simply too many of them; soon, we would be in hand-to-hand combat. Since the REV was dead, we would have to leave it there. Some guys were now stripping it down. Finally, TSgt V yelled, "Get out! Move your asses. Get the fuck out of here!" (Our radios were never very reliable; it was easier, especially in riots, to just yell and use the telephone technique.)

SrA Meade and I began doing a steady backward shuffle; since she was holding the shield, she needed to stay in front. We shuffled back four or five steps, then shot, and repeated this process until we made it out of the area. The detainees ripped through the fencing while the last of us were leaving, but we were far enough away, and they were close enough for the tower guards to use the longer-range riot guns to keep them away from the outer fence. But they couldn't keep them away from our REV. Detainees were pouring into it and screaming like they had won a war. Since it had been stripped down, they couldn't do much to break it; the whole thing is a tracked iron piece of machinery. But they could desecrate it, and they did. Almost a day later, their compound chief got them to stay behind the second fence while we got the REV towed. The inside had urine, blood, feces, and semen smeared all over it; they had used charcoal, rocks, and other pieces of metal to engrave obscene phrases and death threats all over the outside. But crazily enough, once it was taken back to the maintenance shop, the damn thing started right up.

CHAPTER FOURTEEN

MONSTER

T raditionally, May was always a great month for me. Growing up, school always let out in May. I graduated May 17. My military promotions were freakishly in May. I returned home from my first deployment in May. Subconsciously, I used to actually look forward to the month like a good luck charm. But no more.

Growing up in a military community, Memorial Day was always a holiday with a serious meaning behind it. Yes, we might have a church BBQ or family reunion, but most families in the area were quick to teach their children why the holiday existed. The first time I truly understood what Memorial Day was about, my dad answered the phone at our home. I was about nine years old, it was early on a Sunday morning, and he told me to go back to bed as the phone was for my mom, asking her to go to a friend's house. One of the women from our church had just been notified that her husband was killed in Somalia. When I saw her two young sons, I wondered how their world could change so quickly. I then truly began to realize the full meaning of Memorial Day.

On May 9 at Bucca, I had a half day off, so I didn't have to report to work until the chow runner came to pick up dinner. I would meet him at the chow hall and drive into work with him. Taylor had a regular workday, so I still got up at the usual time, and we went and got lunch. Afterward, we headed to the computer stations to see if the line was short enough to get on. It was surprisingly short, so we both got computers almost immediately. We had twenty-minute time limits on the computers, sometimes a little more if no one was in line, which was almost never.

I logged on to my Facebook account, which, back then, was still in its early stages. You could post, comment, message, and update photos—that was pretty much it. I wasn't a huge fan of Facebook, but most of my family used it. So when I did an update, I only had to do one and be done with it. I had a PM from my mom, and a bunch of my friends were posting RIP statuses. I opened the email, and as gently as possible, she said that a friend of mine from childhood, Micah Pierce, had been killed in Iraq. Immediately, my stomach started doing flip-flops, but I was quite confused because he was only sixteen or so.

I told Taylor that I had to get a phone to clear up something, and she got off her computer and came with me too. I miraculously got a hold of a phone and called my parents. My mom answered. I think I may have woken her up; the time zones can really mess with appropriate call times. I told her I had gotten her email, but I thought she was confused. I explained that he was way too young to be in the military, much less Iraq. Delusional thinking was already setting in. She was very patient and told me that he was actually nineteen; his birthday had been just three weeks earlier. She also explained that he had passed on May 6, but there was a little delay due to family notifications. By now, our ten-minute allotment was almost up, and I started saying goodbye. My poor mother wanted to do something to comfort me—a hug or a similar gesture—but she was seven thousand miles away, so a simple "I love you" from each of us would have to do.

Micah was my childhood buddy from our parents' church; his sisters were closer to my age, and I usually played with them more often. I was pretty tomboyish, so at times, Micah and I convinced them to play more boyish games. They lived about a mile from me, and I spent most of one summer rollerblading on their driveway. *The Mighty Ducks 2* had just come out, and we were always reenacting scenes from it. We all went to the same school for a couple of years, and his mom was my teacher for one year. Eventually, they moved away, and we saw them once or twice afterward. We weren't the best friends, but we were close for a little while. He was the first person I knew who was killed in action.

Once I got off the phone, Taylor hugged me tightly; she had only caught bits and pieces of the conversation, but it was clear what was happening. At that moment, I did something that became a habit or reflex ever since. While we were hugging, I started to cry but only for a second. I stopped right away, because somewhere along the line, I began to think that crying was both weak and useless. Crying accomplished nothing. Besides, crying calms anger, and anger was what I relied on to push me through each obstacle. I have always regretted this. Crying is appropriate during loss and is a way of honoring the person that passed. In the past almost fifteen years, I have only cried full out twice—twice, that's it. A subconscious decision made fifteen years ago still affects me every day.

Taylor stayed with me for as long as she could; eventually, she had to go to work. After she left, I went to my pod, thankful that Rahn would be at work. I made it inside, locked the door, and screamed. I yelled, screamed, and punched my wall locker, the door, and the walls for about ten minutes. My monster erupted from the small cage that held it back. My entire being was vibrating with absolute hatred of everything and anything Arabic, Iraqi, Middle Eastern—I despised it all.

From this point on, Heather was asleep when it came to anything

regarding the deployment or Middle Eastern. I was now officially a
monster. The hatred I had before was laughable; I used to think that
hatred was a hot, burning anger. After this metamorphosis, the anger
became icy hot, my fingers and hands vibrated, my mouth spouted
whatever came out, and my heart and soul were numb to emotion or
affection. I relished the idea of hurting detainees; before it was a
means to an end, but now I looked forward to the opportunity to
inflict pain. If those are the core portions of your psyche, then you
have no room for compassion or sympathy; every emotion becomes
twisted into some form of anger and hatred.

This was the culmination of the deployment, loss, and the
uncertainty of when or even if we would leave. I was worn down by
the constant stress of dealing with thousands of people who wanted
Americans dead every moment of the day; now, I was overwhelmed
by the loss of a friend at the hands of those same people. I was a
brand-new NCO, and already, I was officially cracking.

It was almost time to meet up with the chow runner, so I headed
over to the chow hall. I met with A1C Sullivan, a good guy on my
element, who I considered a friend. Now that I was an NCO, our
relationship was a little different, but I still chilled and talked with
him at the smoke pit. We loaded up the food, jumped into the
Humvee, and headed back to the TIF. He was talking about the work
they had done already and some other gossip, but I really wasn't
paying attention. He quieted down after maybe two minutes; finally,
he asked me what was wrong. "Nothing, I'm just thinking," I replied.

"Sarge, I know you. You're never this quiet. Something's
bothering you."

I didn't want to say anything because I irrationally thought if I
didn't talk about it, maybe it wouldn't be true. I was afraid my voice
would crack, and I didn't want to sound weak. But it had to come out.
"I kind of found out a friend of mine died the other day."

"Sgt O'Brien, I'm sorry. What happened?"

"It was an IED somewhere north of here."

"Wait, what? It was a friend from home, and he was deployed too? Shit, that's awful. I'm really sorry."

After that, we rode back to our QRF shack in awkward silence. We had finally moved into the new area away from Compound 6. After setting up the food, I went into the building to see what I needed to do for the day. TSgt V told me that a team was finishing up an intake for a smaller-than-normal group of detainees, so not too many people had to go. He asked me to see if they needed any help finishing up. I got a baton and walked over to the processing area.

Everyone was nearly done. A few detainees in Area 4 were waiting to be picked up or taken to compounds. As I walked around the group, this idea began to unfold. Since some of these guys were newly detained, they might have been in the area when Micah was killed. Hell, they might have even set up the IED. I started asking them, "Where are you from? Where did you get picked up?"

The answer was always the same: "Baghdad." Every detainee will always say that, no matter if they are Egyptian, Somalian, Iranian, or Chechen—the answer is always Baghdad. Part of this is because detainees were bused in from Camp Cropper, which is near Baghdad. It's also because that is their standard answer for interrogation, just like ours would simply be America if they interrogated us.

With each answer of "Baghdad," I grew more frustrated and angry. I had now convinced myself that his killer was here in this group. Finally, after asking two men the same question, they made a sound of tongue-sucking, much like teenagers do when they get an attitude and roll their eyes. But in Iraqi culture, the noise is usually followed with a go-away gesture and the person just turning their head. The meaning is simple and clear: You are nothing, and I am not going to even acknowledge you. This response was common from most detainees to women and made me almost insane with anger on most days.

But this day wasn't like other days, and I was already so worked up that my self-control was pushed to the snapping point. At that noise and gesture from those two detainees, I raised my baton and just started swinging. My vision was cloudy, and I don't even know if I was making noise, but I bet I was. My last semi-coherent thought was, *I want to kill all these motherfuckers. They need to die.* I may have even said that aloud. I have no idea how long I beat them; I just got more and more angry. I would have killed them, I'm certain, if someone hadn't grabbed me and pulled the baton away. I don't know how I got out of Area 4, but suddenly, our QRF Captain was standing in front of me, demanding to know what the hell just happened.

I stared at him, slightly confused. One thought looped through my mind. *Capt. McIntyre* never *comes to any of the in-out processings! Why the hell is he here today?*

He kept grilling me. "SSgt O'Brien, I asked you a question. What the fuck are you doing?"

I stuttered, "I don't know." I knew I was in big shit, but I really didn't care. I didn't quite know what had happened either.

A1C Sullivan came running up. "Sir, SSgt O'Brien just found out that a friend of hers was killed by insurgents three days ago." The captain looked at me and asked if it was true. Still slightly confused, I nodded. He told a couple of airmen to load up the detainees and take them to the TIF hospital to get checked out. The captain then ordered me to go back to QRF and wait for him there. I was not to go on any runs, digs, or searches until he spoke with me. So I walked back to QRF, turned in my baton, and waited for him.

A while later, the captain called me to his office. When I reported to him, TSgt Ewing and TSgt V were in the room. He explained what had happened earlier. He asked me if I remembered what I did. I said yes. He then told me to find a way to get my head straight, and we would just move on from this day.

And I did. Slowly, I got my head right, which, for me, meant staying within the TIF rules but just barely.

From that point on, I actively went out of my way to destroy their property during searches, often taking their toothbrushes and rubbing them in the dirt or on the bottom of my boot. I ripped up any pictures I found and sprinkled the pieces around the tents. One of my personal favorite things to do was take their shampoo and pour it all over their mattresses. When I interacted with them, I told them I hoped they died slowly or called them monkeys or dogs. I intentionally tried to antagonize them so I could respond with violence. I abided by the rules only when it suited me because I didn't want to leave my friends. I didn't even worry about jail because in Bucca, I was already in prison.

"Sgt. O'Brien!" My back tensed; I knew that voice. Sighing inwardly, I turned and waited for TSgt Hai, my squad leader from my home base and my current immediate supervisor, to catch up with me. We didn't see each other too often since he worked Compound 12 where the kids, elderly, and sick stayed. QRF didn't do too many searches there. That was okay with me; he was a difficult NCO, hard-nosed and old school. My first impression of him at Little Rock was when an airman said, "TSgt Hai, I think you hate us." Without missing a beat, he deadpanned, "I do, but I hate you all equally." Later, as we worked together more often and especially by the end of this deployment, I came to have a great deal of respect for him; he was tough, but he made sure to stand up for his people and wouldn't let anyone else correct them but himself.

As he walked up to me, I assumed he wanted to talk about my little episode a few days prior. I wasn't sure how he had found out, but I figured someone told him because he was my supervisor. I got ready for the grilling to begin; one reason he was so intimidating was because he never yelled. In fact, the more pissed he was, the quieter he spoke. The first question he asked me was unexpected. "Do you know SSgt Jason Sand?"

SSgt Sand was a guy from our home base who was currently deployed for a year with another squadron. I knew him only in passing. When he returned from his previous deployment, I was at the Control Desk and had his car keys there. When he came up, we chatted for a few minutes. I had talked to him a few times while he was deployed when he called the desk to be patched through to his parents. He was the only person I knew that had managed to secure a year-long deployment while on a deployment, so occasionally, I asked him about the process. That was our only interaction. "I met him once or twice and spoke with him on the phone a few times. Why?"

For the first time ever, TSgt Hai became a little uncomfortable. "Well, we just found out from headquarters up north that he was killed in action today. The commander wants all the people stationed at Little Rock to try to contact their families today because the news back home will be airing that someone from Little Rock died. But we cannot tell our families who passed, just let them know that we are okay."

Okay. Right, we are all okay. Sure. If there was one thing I learned, it's that I would never be okay again. He continued, "I need you to tell the Little Rock guys on QRF. You know, pass the message along." Numb, I simply nodded. I had just found out another person I knew had been killed by these bastards, and now I had to tell others and make a notification of sorts. As I turned to go, he leaned in and whispered, "I heard about your incident the other day. Frankly, I'm impressed you didn't kill the bastards." And he quietly walked away.

I stumbled back toward my pod, trying to think. I went right over to Taylor's pod, knowing she would be there. I told her what had happened and that she needed to call home and tell other Little Rock troops. I knew she would appreciate how I was feeling. She didn't know SSgt Sand really well either, but he was from our home base and a cop. We all had a brotherhood of sorts that made us grieve even if we didn't know the person. We both sat quietly for a few moments, then headed to lunch and to begin our day.

Once I got to the staging area, I told a couple of the Little Rock guys that we needed to talk as soon as we got to the shack. I told myself that I wanted to try to get everyone together at once, but I really only wanted to delay the inevitable. I didn't know if any of them knew him well. Once we arrived at the QRF shack, I tried to grab a couple of the Little Rock people from the off-going shift before they left. A1C Torrey, one of my troops that I supervised, saw me and said, "SSgt O'Brien, have you talked to TSgt Moore or TSgt Hai today?" I told her I had, and I needed to say something to all of them before they left.

"Don't worry, SSgt O'Brien, TSgt Moore already told us about SSgt Sand." Relieved, I told her thanks, then I would just tell the guys from my shift in a small group. Even though I was her supervisor, she gave me incredibly smart advice. "Don't tell them all together. Guys get weird around each other and will try to act all macho. Tell them individually so they can have a few minutes without others seeing them. Also, SrA Richardson knew him pretty well, I think, just so you're aware." I thanked her for the information and reminded her to call her family and fiancé when she got back to the LSA.

I decided to talk to A1C Bryan first. He didn't know SSgt Sand at all, so while still difficult, it wouldn't be as emotional. We went to a quieter area, and I bluntly told him about SSgt Sand's death. I asked him to please call his family to reassure them that he was okay but not to say anything about who had died. He seemed shocked but understood the whole depth of what I said. He even asked me if I had known him. I said, "Not really, but others here did so keep an eye on the Little Rock people."

Next up was SrA Richardson, all 6'5" and muscled mass, a gentle giant. He even had his wife's face tattooed on his arm, so she was always the first and last thing he saw each day. He had known SSgt

Sand pretty well, but I did not know that they had been roommates on a previous deployment. I tried to approach the whole subject sensitively, but grace isn't really one of my skills. I stumbled and choked for a few seconds until finally I said, "Look, I don't really know how to do this, so I'm just going to say it. SSgt Sand was killed earlier today by an IED. When you get off work tonight, please call your wife and let her know you are okay. The local news channels will be saying someone died, and you don't want her to worry about you. But please do not tell her who it is. The base needs to contact his family first."

Richardson just sat there and looked at me. "Are you sure? It could be another SSgt Sand." I knew that look, understood that thought process.

"I'm sorry, Tom. They wouldn't have told us all this information if it might be someone else. It's definitely him."

I have beaten people, seen a decapitated motorcyclist, and once even arrested a man who beat his cancer-ridden girlfriend, but watching Richardson crumble into tears was one of the worst experiences ever. I just stood there, knowing I couldn't do a single thing. After a few seconds, I awkwardly tried to give him a hug. I asked if he would like some time to himself. He simply nodded. I went back to the shack and told everyone to give him some space.

By now, almost everyone knew what had happened; the information had come down from leadership, and the news spread fast. Like I said earlier, Security Forces isn't the largest group, and even if we didn't know the person, we still had a connection and all grieved. Some people knew SSgt Sand from other deployments, basic training, or tech school. Our QRF Captain, probably remembering how I reacted less than a week earlier, made sure that no Little Rock personnel did any in-processings for a few days. But other than that, we went back to work. Do another search, dig, or riot; the mission still needed to be done.

CHAPTER FIFTEEN

RIOT TO DEATH

T he day started out like a regular workday. The daytime heat now climbed to between 110 and 115, making work all the more enjoyable. (Not!) One side effect was the detainees were too hot to riot anymore. Or so we thought. Right before dusk, we got a call to head to Compound 4 for a possible riot.

When we arrived, the riot was in its earliest stages: some chanting, a few rocks here and there, nothing too serious. But the TIF commander wanted to keep the riots from starting if at all possible. He was under pressure from his leadership to make them end. Apparently, the higher ups weren't too fond of hearing about so many riots each week and the injuries sustained. Also, everyone in the TIF was aware that we didn't want another incident like the one in 2005.

Back in 2005, before the TIF was finished, only c wire held the detainees in place. The TIF had a huge riot that lasted for three straight days and ended when a tower guard finally fired live rounds to stop some detainees from escaping. Five detainees died, but the riot stopped. Some people from that deployment were here on our deployment too. They said it was straight chaos; helicopters were even hovering over compounds to flatten tents on the detainees. It was a miracle no guards were killed. That riot was always in the back of our minds, and I'm sure the TIF commander was constantly worried that with all our overcrowding, it might happen again.

The rioting wasn't too intense at Compound 4 until suddenly it was. Rocks, tent poles turned into javelins, and flaming feces (a new favorite) began raining down instantly. I have no idea what turned the tide, but it went from a wimpy little riot to full-on crazy from that moment on. One of the tower guys, A1C Williams, was given permission to engage groups with our most recent arrival, the M32 weapon. This grenade launcher could shoot five or six rounds before a reload; we lovingly referred to it as the "doom gun." We had even been given extended range rounds; the round was encased in a metal tube for further distance before the rubber crowd rounds dispersed the group of people. Only a few compounds had them. It was still in the testing phase, but none had been used in a riot yet. It was relatively quiet, just a slight *thump* followed by a huge *pop* at the point of impact. That night, A1C Williams was hot; each time they would try to rally up, he blew them apart. It was a beautiful sight.

The biggest point, so far, of the night for me came after the riot intensified. I had been running with my shield guy who was quite a bit taller than me, so he easily outpaced me. We were trying to reach the fence so we could engage with the shotguns. I had slowed down because a group of detainees was hitting the towers with rocks. I was getting ready to fire on them, but the fencing would just deflect all my pellets. That should have been my first thought, but I blame adrenaline. So I lowered my weapon and started running. *Bam!* A perfect rock shot to my vest stunned me so that I stumbled from running to a standstill. If my shotgun and hands had still been up in the firing position, that hit would have easily broken my right hand. My shield guy noticed I wasn't right behind him and stopped. He asked if I was all right. I took about ten seconds to squeak out, "Yeah, just winded!" At the end of the night, I took my bulletproof plate out of my vest; the rock had cracked it right in half! It definitely would have shattered my hand.

While we were at Compound 4, almost the entire rest of the TIF was beginning to riot as well. It was a very developed plan to see if we would be able to stop them and a last-ditch effort for a mass breakout. That night, everybody was pulled and recalled from the TIF, even SSgt Rahn. We did a double-take when we saw each other; by that point, I was so sweaty and filthy, she didn't even recognize me at first.

After a while of firing the doom gun, all the detainees began hunkering down in their huts. They were refusing to go into the holding area. Around this time, Col. Williams, the TIF commander, was driving between the Navy and Air Force sides of the TIF, trying to assess the whole situation. Suddenly, his windshield cracked into a thousand pieces. A well-placed rock had smashed the windshield of one of the few nice, air-conditioned vehicles on the base. Livid, he ordered every detainee in all the compounds into their holding areas. Any compound, quad, or communal that refused was to receive a hard push until everyone complied.

Once our leadership got that message, we began preparing for a hard push on Quad C in Compound 4. Now most of us had done this before, but we had been broken down into teams, and each group knew exactly what to do. We were prepared. Not this time. We were told to get them in their holding area by any means necessary. The people I worked with that night did an amazing job. Many of them were not QRF, some of them weren't even TIF personnel, but they were just the first to respond to the recall.

We formed up. This time, SrA Lowell and I were the team corners for Group B. We were supposed to set up next to one of the huts; each of us threw a grenade in a hut and then let the larger group run around us. We got ready to go in. The guys pulled the cord to the claymores; nothing, neither of them went off. In we ran, claymores be damned! I threw the grenade in the first hut, and SrA Lowell chucked hers into the second hut. I turned with my shield guy but couldn't meet up with Lowell because the whole sixty-man team had run in between our team instead of around us. It split us right in half, which would have been absolutely hilarious if my grenade hadn't accidentally set the hut on fire. My shield woman and I were pressed up against this hut that was going up in flames for maybe ninety seconds. My shield was screaming, "SSgt O'Brien, the shield is melting, the shield is melting!"

I suddenly flashed to the *Wizard of Oz*. "I'm melting, I'm melting." I started laughing so hard, I began choking. Once the team finished running through us, we met back up with Lowell and began clearing the other huts that were still standing. When all the detainees were in their holding area, we began marching out of the compound. Once we got to the Green Mile, we saw the extent of the rioting. Fires were in Compounds 2, 7, and 10 with more smoke billowing up on the Navy side.

My shield woman looked at me. "No offense, Sergeant, but you're nuts! How can you laugh when we were almost burned alive?" I explained the movie reference, but she wasn't that amused. She wandered off, and I found another more reliable shield, someone from my home base who already knew I was a little insane.

We were told to catch our breath and get ready because we were going to be doing this all over the TIF until every detainee complied. As I was resting up and smoking (it's the best way to catch your breath!), a small crowd circled around one small patch of ground. I walked into the group, looked down, and almost tripped over a dead detainee. One side of his face looked completely normal; the other side was dented in. No blood, no gore, just completely caved in as if the bones had been removed. A1C Williams had been very effective with the doom gun. He was in the middle of the group, looking a little ill while we all congratulated him on his shooting. I tried to explain to him that it was like shooting a deer except at least the deer was good for eating. Killing a haji was making the world a better place.

As we were lining up to go to the next compound, I got a new shield, A1C Osbourne. Lucky for me, he was a little on the shorter side. We were told to head over to Compound 10; apparently, the detainees had managed to light one of the guard shacks on fire. Initial rumors were also that detainees were loose in the area and attacking guards; thankfully, that rumor was bullshit. I got a little worried about Taylor; 10 was her compound, and if bad shit were happening, she would be right there in the middle of it. Luckily, I saw her almost immediately when we reached Compound 10.

The whole group of us had simply walked from Compound 4 to 10. There never seemed to be any vehicles around when we needed them. As we arrived, Col. Williams was there as well. Apparently, the rock that hit his truck had come out of Compound 10, and boy, was he mad as hell! We lined up to enter Quad D; thankfully, this time, the claymores actually worked and exploded on time. In we rushed. Lowell and I both got our grenades off successfully. We didn't get separated either; everything was running smoothly. And then one of the huts caught on fire again. We were ordered to try to put it out. I've never had that order given before or since, so I guess it came from Col. Williams. He was what we called a detainee lover, always trying to quell riots with treats and compromise. In came some firefighters with the long hose, and A1C Osbourne and I were told to escort them as closely as possible to the firefighters and provide protection.

So we begin walking and creeping closer and closer to the hut. We didn't seem too close, but it was really smoky, and I couldn't tell if any detainees were around, so we kept going. Suddenly, it felt as if the firefighters were spraying me. A cold wonderful sensation started at the crown of my head and just poured through my body. It felt like the best shower I've had in months! A firefighter suddenly grabbed

Osbourne and me. "You guys can't get any closer. Your shield is starting to melt!"

Apparently, that beautiful cooling feeling was because my body was getting so hot that my sweat began to feel cold and work in overdrive. So in one night, I melted two shields and had a second and third close encounter with fire. Seriously, what is it with me and fire?

Once we finished up in Quad D, we headed over to Quad B. By this point, it was nearly 2300 hours; we had been doing this since about 1600 hours. We were hitting the point of exhaustion, especially the teams that kept running into the quads and dragging detainees to their holding areas. At each compound, before we went in, the towers were releasing massive amounts of gas grenades. I had stopped using my gas mask after the first one because it got contaminated with gas sealed into it, making it worthless. So each time, I was getting hit with the gas as was most everyone else. Another side effect of the gas is that it works on your pores as they open up. When you begin to sweat, the burning creeps through your body, and I do mean all of your body. My eyes had stopped burning, but my armpits and sides were on fire. If the burn hit any other areas, I wouldn't be able to keep going. As we got ready to hit Quad B, this was the last one I could do. If we had to do anymore, I would tap out.

Grenades out! Gas misted the area. Boom! Both claymores worked beautifully. In we ran! Lowell's grenade went flying into the first hut; mine went into the next one. Our team held the line; Group C ran by with no splitting in the middle. This time, neither of our grenades lit huts on fire. The third time was a charm. The majority of detainees in other parts of the TIF were finally calming down. They realized that we would push everyone if they kept it up. Plus, the other compounds had been battling it out for hours as well; they fought to reclaim their compounds and won. Finally, we were catching a break; the detainees were either beaten or just as exhausted as we were, and the rioting slowly began to end.

I ran into Taylor right outside her compound; we chatted for a few minutes, and she told me all about how their guard shack went up in flames from a lucky shot: either a flaming orange or a flaming poop bomb. We chuckled about it for a little while, then QRF had to load up and head back to our shack. Once we arrived, we did a quick debrief, conducted accountability, turned in our shotguns and shields, and prepared to head back to the LSA.

Driving out of the TIF that night was wild. The whole base had been on lockdown, and now that it was lifted, all the compounds were doing changeover and driving out at the same time. In addition to that, all the recalled LSA people were waiting to be let back out. Humvees, five-tons, and deuces were stacked all the way up the Green Mile. We made the best of it, though, yelling and shouting to each other all up and down the Mile. It was a tired-party atmosphere.

When I finally got home, I wouldn't even go into the pod; instead, I asked Rahn to just throw me my shower kit and some clothes. I headed right to the shower cadillac and took a seven-minute shower. Oh, luxury! Our showers generally only lasted five minutes at the most. It felt wonderful though, and even though I really wasn't, I felt clean, but only for a moment. Even though I hung my clothes outside that night, the minute I walked into our pod, Rahn still said, "Jesus, Heather! I thought you said you were going to shower!"

The detainee riots were over, but the war with their stench won that night.

CHAPTER SIXTEEN

JUNE 9TH

"Heather. Heather. O'Brien, Heather O'Brien!" As someone shouted my name outside the chow hall, I looked around, trying to see who was calling me. I had just stepped outside and hadn't yet put my sunglasses on; therefore, I was temporarily blinded. A part of me wondered at how pitiful I was that I hadn't paid any attention until I heard my last name; at this point, only Taylor and Rahn used my first name and only occasionally. Other than that, it had been months since I'd heard it. Finally, I spotted a guy walking toward me; I didn't recognize him, but I figured I was about to be yelled at for something. As he got closer, I noticed the Army patches and finally his rank: O-4, a Major.

I snapped a salute while thinking, *Dammit. What did I do this time*?

He saluted back and smiled. "You don't recognize me?"

He took off his hat, and suddenly, I did. "Mr. Phil! I mean, Major Reaux! What are you doing here?"

"Same as you. I got deployed."

Phil Reaux was a member of my parents' church back in Missouri.

I hadn't seen the family in quite a few years, so imagine my surprise when I ran into him in Iraq. He wasn't the only person I would see from back home; I ran into an airman and a Navy sailor from high school. But seeing someone from my old church was a double-edged sword. It was great to talk and catch up with home: who had moved, how big the kids were, etc. On the other hand, it was hard to hear about life going on there without me. Plus, talking about home made my anger cool down, at least temporarily, and a small bubble of hope slowly rose. I hated that bubble of hope.

Maj Reaux was working in the TIF hospital, so I could see him occasionally. One evening, I went down to visit him, and we chatted for a while. I told him about some of the riots, escapes, and other shit. "But don't worry. It's so hot now that they have quieted down. Nothing too crazy has happened for a while, and I don't think they will try anything until it cools down again." It was the night of June 8.

The next morning, Rahn's voice slowly pierced my sleepy haze. "O'Brien, get up and get on the floor." What was she saying? It made absolutely no sense to my exhausted mind.

"'What?" I managed to croak out.

"Get up and get on th—" *Wham! Boom!* Instantly, my body reacted, and I rolled off the bed and onto the ground.

"What the hell was that?" I yelled.

"I think we're getting mortared, and they are actually close this time." Sure enough, a minute later, another explosion went off but a little farther away this time. As we began to dress and gear up, Rahn told me that I had actually slept through two of them. The third one was the first one I heard.

We knew we would be hunkered down for a bit, so we got slowly ready. The Iraqis had terrible aim when it came to our base, so, honestly, at this point, we weren't really concerned. At a knock on the door, there stood Taylor; she was alone in her pod and decided to come over and hang out. We turned my iPod on and started goofing off while waiting for the all clear. Finally, we heard the overhead: "All Personnel Report for Accountability." We got our gear ready to head over to our reporting area. I looked at Taylor. "Where's your helmet?"

"Oh shit, I forgot it in my pod!" She laughed and ran back to get it. I stepped outside, and the unbearable heat hit me like an inferno. It was only around 0820. Later, I would find out the heat index was somewhere around 135 degrees. It was so hot, I could take off my DCU top and wring out my sweat like water. Iraq is always windy, like a hot oven door constantly open. On June 9, there wasn't a single breath of air; even the weather hated us in Iraq.

As Taylor rounded the corner coming back from her pod, the loudspeaker announced, "All medical personnel, report to the TIF. All medical personnel, report to the TIF." We immediately stopped smiling and laughing. We thought the rockets hit near the base, not actually on it. We started jogging toward the reporting area when I realized I didn't have my soft hat, just my helmet. "Shit, Taylor, I gotta go back and get my hat. Go ahead, I'll catch up."

She nodded and kept going while I ran back and grabbed my hat and a water bottle, just in case. As I headed toward the reporting area, people were coming from there. One of them said they were walking to the TIF because all the vehicles were either full or being used. So I started heading that way. As we cleared the pod area, totally white smoke was coming from the TIF, different from the usual black riot smoke. Even though it was only a little over a mile away, it felt as if the walk took forever due to the heat. Finally, I took off my helmet and attached it to my flak vest which I opened. I instantly felt as if the temperature dropped 85 degrees. A white truck drove by and a higher-ranking officer (they were the only ones who had air-conditioned white trucks) yelled out his window, "Hey, Airman, get your helmet on and fix your vest."

Thankfully, he continued to drive and choke us with his dust, or else he might have seen the hand "salute" I gave him. Honestly, though, if another rocket or a mortar hit, my crappy helmet wouldn't do anything, and the plate in my flak vest was already cracked in half —it couldn't possibly work correctly either.

Only one side of the TIF was open, the gate farthest from QRF, but I could see which area had been hit. During the walk, I kept hearing different rumors: various compounds were hit, detainees were free everywhere, nobody knew who was hurt or killed, etc. Each rumor sounded worse than the one before it, so finally, I just shut them out. They were walking to the TIF just like me. What the hell did they know?

Entering the TIF was like entering the twilight zone; normally it's loud with detainees and guards yelling, the occasional shotgun crack, and thousands of people milling about. But that day, it was quiet. At each compound, almost all the detainees were in their huts with no yelling. Finally, on the Green Mile, I could see where the smoke was hovering: Compound 8.

My stomach dropped, and my throat grew tight; my buddy, TSgt Holmes, ran the day shift group at Compound 8. I hustled down there; as I got closer, I started to slow down, beginning to get scared. Carnage was all over that side of the Mile. Injured detainees were laying out on the ground with medics while some TIF guys attended them. It was a mix of different compound guards and five or six QRF guys. Most of the detainees had been transported, but some were still left; some had no arms or legs or cuts to the stomach, back, etc., and of course, there was the row of the obviously dead. In the fencing were parts of what looked like brain, complete with some skull attached, pushed through the links. I was searching for TSgt Holmes. One of my QRF guys kept calling me. I still had to check in with my leadership. I snapped at him to shut the hell up. I was torn—I knew I needed to check in, but I wanted to check on my friend. Finally, I saw SrA Boyd and ran up to her and asked if she had seen TSgt Holmes. "Yes, she is physically okay."

I had no idea why she said it that way, but at least I knew she was all right, and I headed off to the QRF shack. Once there, I almost collapsed from heat. It was now so hot that if I went inside the air-conditioned building, the difference in temperatures between the inside and outside would make me physically ill. I checked in with TSgt V and asked what he needed us to do. He said to get a few more guys from our shift and relieve some of the QRF guys who had been doing an in-processing when the attack occurred. They needed to return to the shack and be accounted for. I took a few guys, and we went over to the in-processing area. All the detainees were in Area 4; they had been waiting for the compounds to pick them up when the rocket hit. The other group left, and we took over the quietest group of detainees I have ever dealt with: no complaints of heat, no insults, no spitting, nothing. These guys were terrified—you could see it in the way they were sitting, trying to get as close to the ground as possible. While they held no love for the infidel Americans, they seemed astounded that their own insurgents would bomb them.

We didn't stay too long; the compounds quickly picked up their new detainees. After the last group left, we headed back to the shack. Apparently, we were just in time—our QRF shift was going back to the LSA for an hour and a half to get some lunch, and then we would relieve the day shift. This time, we got to ride in our vehicles. As soon as we got back to the LSA, I dropped my gear off in my pod and headed over to Taylor's and TSgt Holmes's pod, hoping they were there.

People were moving around in their pod as I got to the front door. I knocked, and Taylor opened the door. TSgt Holmes was sitting on her bed, and I walked over to her. "Thank God, you're okay! I was looking for you down at 8 but had to go to QRF. I was so worried!"

The minute she looked up at me, I knew something wasn't right. Her eyes were totally vacant. The words "She is physically okay" began repeating in my head; now I realized Boyd was differentiating between physical and mental well-being. I looked up at Taylor. "What happened?"

"A concussion, probably. We are going to get lunch and then go to the LSA hospital." Taylor had been assigned by leadership to stay with TSgt Holmes for the next couple of days while she was being medically cleared.

I went with them to lunch. Throughout our conversations, we had to remind TSgt Holmes of different information: training topics, training locations, why she had to go to the hospital, etc. I told them after lunch that I had to head back to work, and she was utterly confused about why I was leaving. I had already told her three times in the past twenty minutes. She definitely had a concussion and the beginnings of a traumatic brain injury. In true military fashion, after about three or four days, the LSA medics cleared her to return to duty.

TSgt Holmes was the closest person to the rocket that didn't suffer major physical trauma. One of the detainees that she had just talked to right before the rocket attack was killed by shrapnel. Now I hated the detainees, but even I realized that having the last one you talked to suddenly turn into pink mist in front of you will fuck up your head for a while. For years, the only memories she had of June 9 were what she was repeatedly told. Some of her memories are now making their way back—fifteen years later.

For the majority of the day, we stayed at our QRF shack. It was so damn hot that even going to the bathroom was awful. The Porta Johns were at least 15 degrees hotter than outside; I went once and had to exit to get my pants back up. They kept sticking to my legs. Later in the evening, we did a simple dig at a compound in an effort to make the time go by. We weren't seriously looking for contraband.

CNN was the first news station to start reporting about the attack, which I found hilarious. We had absolutely no news networks or embedded reporters in Bucca, so how did they know what happened?

But in true CNN fashion, they got it wrong and told everyone watching that many Americans were injured and some might have died. My poor grandmother was watching; they almost gave her a heart attack. Thankfully, I was able to get a hold of my parents within the next day or so, and while I couldn't call my grandmother, at least they could pass on the message.

We got lucky on June 9. No Americans were physically injured. The rockets that hit our LSA missed all the pods and tents, instead hitting the only clear area on base. It was cleared out in order to put in more living quarters, but none had been built yet. For the rest of our deployment, none ever hit inside our perimeter again. A few hit right after we left—like three days later—but as far as I know, no Americans were injured. Eight detainees died from the rockets: Six, almost immediately, and two, over the next couple of days. I chuckle, thinking about the one time they actually hit us and still managed to kill their own people.

Later, we found out how the actual attack was done. An ICO had a GPS unit and set up the tracking on it when he was in the compound. He was supposed to have set it up either at the ICO camp or at our LSA if possible. But he set it up in the TIF instead. The only reason he might have done this is because Compound 8 held a large number of Saddam's former high-ranking military members. Most of the Shia terror groups hated them as much as we did. The ICOs we were supposed to train and depend on had proven yet again why we could never trust them.

CHAPTER SEVENTEEN

EXTENDED AGAIN, HUNGRY, AND INSANE

W e had a new problem at Bucca that had nothing to do with the detainees. We were hungry. The convoys coming from Camp Navistar had been routinely attacked, so the military had re-routed them. Instead of being one of the first camps to get food, we were now one of the last. That meant that the good food was generally already gone, but the real issue was that during the three weeks of convoy re-routing, no food was coming in. But plenty of people were arriving almost daily, so the amount of food went down, but the number of people went up.

Of course, we could always eat at Subway or Pizza Hut. I had learned early in my deployment that Subway was questionable at best. They got resupplied whenever we did, so when the trips became longer, the meat and cheese stayed on the road longer. Let's just say Subway's Eat Fresh motto did not apply at Bucca. Pizza Hut was a little better, but again, no resupply meant no Pizza Hut food either. The BX quickly sold out of their beef jerky and the few small canned items they had.

We never completely ran out of food, thankfully, but it did make for some interesting meals, if you could call them that. My favorite was rice and crushed tomatoes with extra water to make the juice stretch. Not too bad except for one small problem: no utensils. Plastic ware was also on the mythical resupply convoy.

But guess who got fresh food and fruits at every meal? Our lovely detainees at the TIF and in the Hastys got three meals a day; one meal was usually a sandwich, and the other two were hot meals. With each meal, they were also given two oranges and milk. At breakfast and dinner, they received orange juice. Our chow hall hadn't seen fresh fruit in ages unless canned fruit counted.

In the whole scheme of things, fresh food and fruit for the detainees wasn't the worst thing, but when the inmates got food before our own service people, that sent a clear message. Clearly, our government cared more about the well-being of terrorists than of those carrying out the mission. It was just another proverbial punch in the gut. But that wasn't the worst hit they would give us.

We were cruising through June. The riots had really settled down for two major reasons: 1) The first Hastys were finally built and taking detainees. Some of the overcrowding was beginning to slow down. 2) It was so hot, even the Iraqis didn't want to set fires anymore. But we sensed that things were finally coming to an end; the November crew was beginning to pack up some of their stuff and waiting to find out fly dates. We even had a kind of goodbye get together, took photos, and hung out. They were ready to go.

One day, we were alerted to a Commander's Call right after work. All Commander's Calls are mandatory, so we wondered why our leadership insisted and stressed that we be there. Either way, it didn't sound good, and rumors began immediately.

While standing at the platform area with my entire QRF shift, I felt oddly nervous, as if I had done something wrong. First, Lt. Col. Shell introduced a psych doctor who had come in from Kuwait. *That can't be good if they have a crazy doctor here, but what is one doctor going to do for more than five hundred people?* I thought. After that, Lt. Col. Shell delivered the final punch. The November crew was being extended until October or later. My crew, the February crew, was still scheduled to leave in August. He quickly continued. Leadership was working on a way to fix the situation, and all the chaplains were also available if anyone needed them.

We were all crushed. The November guys had reached their limit —they were done. Those of us in the February group felt it was incredibly unfair that they should be extended when they had already been there the longest. Sure enough, about three days later, Lt. Col. Shell had another briefing; now the November crew would leave in August (not October), and the February crew was extended until at least October. The announcement did little to lift morale. It was nice that the November crew was going home first; it was really the only fair option. But it sucked that we would be there until they no longer needed us. At this point, our whole deployed group was taken off our home unit rosters and placed in the Army's deployment personnel rosters. From then on, we no longer existed to our home bases; the Air Force just let us go.

Many of us felt as if the Air Force had discarded us; our military branch just gave us up. It would get worse when, later on, an Air Force Lt. Col. ran into us at the Hastys and had no idea who we were or how long we had been there. By then, we truly felt like bastard children, not even wanted by our own branch of service.

Later that evening, when I got back to my pod, Rahn was there. I felt really bad for her. I had already convinced myself that I would never leave Bucca, but she was a single mother. This was the first time she had been separated from her son, and it had just gotten longer. She seemed pretty upset, and I went over to talk with her.

She just kept saying, "I'm so pissed. It's not fair. All this is wrong. So wrong."

I said, "Yeah, it's fucked up, but it'll end someday. It has to."

"No, you don't understand. You guys, not the headquarters team, got extended for your deployment."

"Rahn, what do you mean? You're leaving here on time?"

"The headquarters group will still leave next month because the new headquarters team will be here." Apparently, during his Commander's Call, Lt. Col. Shell had conveniently forgotten to tell us that he, our First Sergeant, and our Chief, along with their clerks, which included Rahn, would still be leaving in July.

So not only had we been forgotten by the Air Force, but now our commander and all our leadership were leaving us. Around this point, I simply said, "Screw the Air Force." I kept that mentality until the day I left the military. I couldn't understand how our commander could just up and leave without making sure we were taken care of. The notion that our leadership was leaving us didn't sit well with anybody. Nasty letters were slipped under his door, and a mean comic was left on the bulletin board; even the lower-ranking officers and mid-level NCOs were pissed. With that anger came a complete lack of respect for the incoming leadership, which was only bolstered by their lack of knowledge. A common saying was, "What the fuck are you going to do about it? Send me to Iraq?" However, most of us had a great deal of respect for the mid-level NCOs because they were doing the same jobs as us; they were truly leading by example.

I was angry with our leadership, especially Lt. Col. Shell, for years. I thought he should have refused to leave, but really, what would that have done? It would have simply ended his career. He might have been charged with Failure to Obey a Lawful Order, possibly demoted, and probably forced to retire early. Even if he refused, he still would have been forced to leave after being punished. I understand that now, but it took me a long time. I wonder just how hard it must have been to follow that order and then have the people you cared about turn on you and hate you.

One evening, as we were waiting for the vehicles to bring our relief out, I was sitting off by myself. Before our other shift showed up, we always got our weapons out of the armory. So I had my M4 and M9, and I was checking over my M4, debating whether I needed to clean it that night. Neither of the weapons were loaded, but as I was inspecting my M4, I casually lifted it toward Compound 18, about two hundred yards away. I was checking my sights, at least at first, but before I even realized it, I was picking out which detainees I could hit. I began thinking about how many I could shoot before someone realized where the shots were coming from. Right then, Eliza slapped my shoulder. "Hey, bud! Whatcha doing?"

Still a little intrigued with my idea, I told her, "Just sitting here, thinking about how many of those fuckers I could shoot before I got caught."

For a few minutes, Eliza didn't say a word. Then she slowly changed the subject. She sat with me until the vehicles came, and we headed home for the night. Now I didn't plan to do anything, but in true SSgt Orleans fashion, she stayed around and made sure I'd be okay. If she had told any of our higher ups, I would have immediately been relieved of duty, especially after the whole beating of the detainees, but she didn't say a word. She was a friend and watched out for me.

A group of us—TSgt Holmes, Taylor, SrA Boyd, and sometimes a few others—gathered outside Taylor's and Holmes's pod. We sat on lawn chairs and talked or listened to music, trying to do something semi-normal. Even here, I was beginning to feel out of place. I got into arguments with Holmes and Taylor regarding my ideas of how the detainees should be treated. I felt as if we should take a couple of them out of each compound and make the others watch while we had a dog bite them (a big no-no in Muslim culture) and then shoot them in the head before they were able to cleanse themselves or conduct prayer. Then we would tell the others if they still refused to comply with our orders, we would continue doing this every thirty minutes.

They argued I was crossing a line; I argued it would work to keep the others in line. At one point, I got so angry with them, I had to leave for the night.

Another time, TSgt Holmes mentioned that a few Americans were somewhere in her compound. They had actually left the United States to come and fight us in Iraq. I was completely stunned. People like that existed in my country? She did say she didn't know who they were but that according to intel, there were some. I told her never to tell me who they were. She said she wouldn't and asked why. "Because I will kill them. And I don't care what punishment I get. I will kill any Americans imprisoned here if I find them."

I meant it too. The idea of fighting in Iraq with the insurgents made them traitors, and traitors deserved death.

I had accepted that I would never leave Bucca. It was now more real to me than home. I was even kind of standoffish with people from our home base. Our relief unit had finally arrived, except we weren't leaving but staying with them and the November crew. At the chow hall, I ran into a few guys from the relief unit who were from my base and talked with them for a few minutes. They kept telling me about stuff happening back home. After a few minutes, I finally said, "Look, I don't give a shit about Little Rock. They let the Army just take us for as long as they want. So Little Rock can just go fuck themselves."

I walked away, so angry; I couldn't believe that these guys didn't understand why I was so pissed. But how would they have known? They hadn't been here when we were extended time and time again. They didn't know that we were stuck here until, well, whenever. But I didn't care—I simply felt angry with almost everyone. The monster was now beginning to alienate me from the people I cared about.

CHAPTER EIGHTEEN

GOODBYES ALL AROUND

"Hey, everybody, listen up! There is a list of people who will be going to Hasty 31 and 32. You will be reporting there tomorrow. The pickup area is the same as QRF for now. I'll read off the names and post the list inside. Listen for your name." TSgt V's announcement wasn't a surprise, but it still felt as if our little family were being ripped apart. Just another reason to dislike the new guys at QRF.

The June crew with more than four hundred people had officially arrived for a full deployment. They started working with us; so far, the blending of the groups had been rocky at best. When our group had arrived, the prison was so hectic and violent that it had helped our crew and the November crew mesh. Plus, at that time, morale was still pretty high. So far, with the June crew, we had a few shouting matches, but soon, a fight might break out. It wasn't entirely their fault; they were coming into a well-oiled—and a pissed-off—machine. We honestly never gave them a chance.

The last straw was when we went to do a dig. Most of us stayed behind and let the June crew and a few of our guys go. They were supposed to relieve my crew. QRF was suddenly full with almost two shifts of people. So these guys took about six–eight older members and went to the dig. A few hours later, when they came back, people were screaming at each other before the trucks even stopped rolling. I went over to see what the problem was, and SrA Lowell was yelling at another SrA about almost getting them killed. She was livid, and shockingly, so was SSgt Orleans. I had never seen her this pissed off; she was red and muttering to herself. I asked her what happened, and she said, "They almost got us killed! I trained these assholes myself, and the first time they do a dig, they try to kill us!"

I finally managed to get the whole story out of them although it took a while to calm them down enough to talk. Apparently, in a show of wanting to let the older crew have an easier time, the new guys decided they would do all the digging and the older guys would just hold the line. Holding the line was relatively simple; we would go in and stand in between the fencing that keeps the detainees in the holding area separated from their living area. Each person on the line has a shotgun; they are the first group in and the last group to leave before the detainees are released back into their living area. It's their responsibility to check the huts and tents to make sure everyone is out before leaving and allowing the detainees to come back. The whole dig went fine until the end. Apparently, due to some miscommunication, the new guys allowed the detainees to begin entering the area before the line guys left. Many of us had had nightmares about this: being locked in an area with more than 350 detainees all rushing in. Thankfully, nobody was hurt, and they managed to get out safely, but nobody wanted to work with the new guys anymore.

A couple of days later, TSgt V made his announcement. We had heard rumors that we would be taking over some of the new Hasty compounds. My jaw dropped—almost all my friends were going, and I was not on the list. I was staying in QRF without my entire element,

Flight Sergeant, and most of the other NCOs. Later that day, I went to the new officer in charge. Capt. McIntyre had been relieved to go home as part of the command element. Instead, we had a new First Lieutenant; I explained to him that I would prefer to go to Hasty 31 and 32 instead of staying in QRF. I told him I was burned out with the duties and didn't want to make a mistake because of it. He seemed pretty dismissive and simply told me he would think about it.

The first day without the crew was awful. I felt like the new kid in school but also like a kid who was repeating the same grade for the fifteenth time. A couple of us were still together: A1C Sullivan, Copeland, and a few others. The next day, the First Lt. called me into the shack and told me I would be reporting to the Hastys the following day. I thanked him and went outside to tell Sullivan and Copeland; they were a little upset but understood why I needed to leave. Soon, they ended up out there as well.

Initially, when I began at the Hastys, they weren't fully built yet. The Hastys are comprised of HESCOs, which are gargantuan green-gray barriers that stand up and are filled with soil or sand to set them in place. A HESCO barrier is approximately eight- to ten-feet tall and maybe four-feet wide; we had them placed three thick and three high. Instead of fencing, we had the HESCOs, and all along the top and bottom, we strung C-wire with razor wire inside the C-wire. It was pretty interesting getting the razor wire placed inside the C-wire strands; initially, we had a guy crawling around in the C-wire, but he got razor wire caught in his thigh and had to be taken to the medical facility. He was millimeters from nicking his femoral artery. After that, we had a much smaller female do all the crawling around. Even our towers were rapidly built. They were wooden with no glass or plastic in the windows. In fact, nothing at all was in the windows. The top of the towers was covered with some sunshades to try to keep the heat down.

The best part was that no detainees were in the Hastys because the compounds weren't ready yet. For about a week or so, we just reported to work and spent the day fortifying and preparing the compounds.

The Hasty compounds were much different than the regular compounds. For one, they weren't in the actual TIF; in fact, they were built outside it, next to the final berm of the camp. The final berm is the last wall of the base; it had towers every few hundred meters, and the guards up there only fired lethal weapons. In essence, if a detainee escaped the Hastys and headed toward the berm, he would be killed with no warning. Since they were not in the TIF proper, the Hastys were smaller than regular compounds and had only two quads that held about two hundred detainees. The quads were side by side with HESCOs separating them.

At each quad was a vehicle gate that we used to get the water tank in and out of their holding area twice a day. We wrapped the interior of that gate with many strands of C-wire and razor wire. We also created another observation spot right next to the gate. It was on top of a storage pod with no building or safety in case of a riot, just a sunshade and a chair. But from that spot, we could easily see the entire holding area; the only spot that was not immediately visible was at the base of the pod. We would have to walk to the edge and look straight down in order to check down there.

There was only one gate (besides the truck gate) in and out of each quad where the detainees walked from their living area into their holding area. They would have to funnel down a narrow walkway to ensure they couldn't gang up and rush the gates, then go through a cage-type walkway into the holding area. The door was right at the beginning of the cage; a person was also posted on top of the gate during head count and anytime the gate was being opened. We called that post the shark cage, because that's what the whole cage resembled. I loved working the shark cage but was always a little worried that the detainees would try to stab my feet through the slits. It happened a few times in other compounds.

The Hastys were created because the TIF proper was bursting at the seams. We kept getting more and more detainees with absolutely no place to put them. Bucca was technically overcrowded when we arrived in January; as I mentioned earlier, by now, we had more than twenty thousand people in a place built for five thousand. Since the Hastys were so rudimentary and lacking in any amenities for the detainees, Col. Williams had decided that only the problem detainees would be put in them. Inside the TIF, the detainees had access to giant TVs, movies, air-conditioned shacks (when they didn't burn them down), and separated and closed showering and bathroom facilities. The Hastys didn't have any of that. The detainees lived there in tents with no TV at all, and their bathrooms were Porta Johns that were cleaned once a day. They also had one water tank per quad that was filled twice a day as long as we weren't too busy. We searched their living areas each shift because they were problem detainees.

Problem detainees were terrorists who tried to radicalize anyone they could. They incited riots, attempted escapes, or beat other inmates, sometimes killing them. They deserved to be out here with us, we who had given up hope of ever leaving. The combination of violent inmates and hopeless and angry guards made for many fun times. But for now, we didn't have any of them; we were still building and securing the compounds.

And then one day, we did. I had arrived at work right as the last of a group of detainees was coming off the bus. Not many were there yet, only around ninety or so and only in Quad A. That very first shift, I realized this would be much different from QRF. We were now expected to build a rapport with a bunch of guys who hated QRF. It would be interesting, to say the least.

Learning to work and interact with the detainees as compound guards and not QRF was quite a challenge. Standard operating procedure was to react quickly and decisively whenever a detainee didn't follow instructions. The reasoning behind this was that many times, we were in the holding areas at in- or out-processing. They easily outnumbered us ten to one at all times. In addition, we wanted the detainees to think of QRF as the punishment for any of their infractions; we wanted them to dislike our presence at their compounds. So we were used to dealing with rioting or violent detainees, but it was totally different dealing with detainees who were not necessarily rioting but who were deemed too violent for the TIF. In short, we had no set procedure for dealing with them; we were supposed to make up the rules as we went along.

For the most part, we learned through trial and error how to safely get things done. During my shift, we had to give the detainees their dinner, which was dumped off near their front entry an hour or two before dinnertime. It was wrapped in plastic, and the fruit always came in crates. Well, none of that was allowed in the quads; we had a special food crew of detainees who were responsible for coming out and bringing their own containers to carry the food in.

On my first day of Hasty food duty, I had no idea who the food crew was, so I had the compound interpreter (a detainee who speaks English, not to be confused with an ICO interpreter) come out with the food guys. They got all the food in their containers, broke all the boxes down, and bagged them up. Then, all the food crew turned to go back inside except one guy, who grabbed the trash and just nonchalantly walked away. A couple of guys yelled at him, and we chased him. The first guy to reach him sprayed him, and another used his baton to arm bar the guy back toward the quad. Meanwhile, the interpreter was yelling at us in half English, half Arabic. We later learned he was just going to throw the trash away. In his old compound, their crew was responsible for taking the trash to the dumpsters. Our dumpsters were a good four hundred yards away from the compound entry, so that was out of the question. Just another new detail to work out.

We quickly figured out that we could get the detainees to do their mandatory evening head count by not allowing their food crew to get the food until the head count was done. After that, we locked them in their holding area, and while they ate dinner, we searched their living area. This was an easy enough routine to stick to, but no, the detainees always angled to get their food earlier, avoid head count, etc. The easiest way to get them lined up was to simply say, "No head count, no food." If they didn't believe me, after a few minutes, I began passing out their fruit, mostly oranges, to our tower guards and rovers. Our food lines were still disrupted, and we hadn't had fresh fruit in months. Yet somehow, they did—it only seemed fair to share the wealth.

At the beginning of August, the November crew was finally heading home. It was incredibly bittersweet; I was really happy for them, yet I had gotten closer to many of them and knew their reactions better than my own team members. Plus, my roommate, SSgt Rahn, was heading home, too, as a part of our leadership team. In a cruel twist, I found out right as she was leaving that I also had to vacate my pod so higher-ranking NCOs could take it. Because of the damn surge, more people were crawling all over base, and now the higher ranks wanted better accommodations, which meant we were kicked out of our homes and pushed other lower ranks out of theirs. So in twenty-four hours, many of my buddies left, Rahn left, and I was kicked out of what had been my home for the past seven months. It sucked.

My new living area was a four-man hut far away from most of the recreational areas and uncomfortably close to where the rockets had hit in June. I was about a half mile from where I used to live, which meant it was a lot harder for me to see TSgt Holmes. However, one of my new roommates included Taylor, which was great. My other two roommates were equally awesome: SSgt Gina Eloy, who was quiet until I got to know her, and SSgt Calvin, whose personality far outmatched her tiny size. Man, what a spitfire! She drove around the TIF in a Humvee and needed to sit on a phone book to see over the hood. Gina and I once watched the movie *Knocked Up* at my old pod. We were laughing until it got to the point where they showed the birth of the baby. We both yelled and tried to fast forward the movie. After it was over, Gina dryly said, "I can never unsee that." It still makes me laugh.

Now that the November crew was gone, our group at the Hastys was pretty small; leadership decided to give us more people from my team. Only people from my team were working in the Hastys; none of the newer June crew was out there. My new shift sergeant was none other than TSgt Hai. I was initially less than thrilled. But Taylor was moved from Compound 10 out to the Hastys Tactical Operations Center (TOC) and worked at 31 once or twice a week. That meant I got to harass her over the radio. Hasty 32's new shift leader was TSgt Holmes, so I was finally able to chat with her more easily again.

These were bittersweet reunions. It was great to be with my buddies again, but a part of me still really missed our November crew. Both of our crews had been through a lot together, and it felt weird to be at Bucca without them, like when a sibling moves out of the house. Life at Bucca just wasn't the same.

CHAPTER NINETEEN

ROCKET MAN AND SHIT EVERYWHERE

E ventually, we began to get more detainees from outside Bucca. We had no more room in the TIF, so instead of having only problem detainees, we occasionally got new or older ones. If the detainee was older or in bad health, they were usually moved pretty quickly to Compound 12 for the infirmed inside the TIF. We got new detainees almost daily and had to sift through who was healthy enough to be housed in the Hastys. As such, we had some really interesting characters show up.

One day, a group came in and was getting off the bus. An old guy was riding piggyback on this quite large young male. Immediately, I told the interpreter to have the old man get down; we didn't do that here. He translated, and the old man slid off the younger one and sat on the ground. Now a little pissed, I yelled at him to get up and start walking. He began to talk rapidly and motioned to his back. The interpreter told me, "He is paralyzed, and the man carrying him is his nephew."

Now I was interested. "Ask him how he got arrested if he is paralyzed."

"He says he was out after curfew, and when the soldiers showed up, his friends left him in his wheelchair on the street." What a beautiful example of true friendship! Needless to say, he was moved to Compound 12 that day.

Another day, a detainee came in who had been stapled back together. Frankenstein had nothing on this guy. His staples began at his feet and ran up the full length of his body, including his arms. I escorted him to the medic tent to have them removed because they had been in so long, skin was growing over in some areas. He didn't speak English very well, and since we needed a translator the whole time he was in the medic tent, we found another detainee to do the translating. This way, our ICO translator was free to move around the compounds since he covered more than one.

My curiosity was killing me, so I asked the guy what happened to him. The interpreter translated, and the detainee replied, "America . . . Boom!" while making frantic motions of a small square with a triangle on top and then them blowing apart.

The translator said, "He says you Americans blew up his house." He glared at us.

"We blew his house up for no reason."

"Yes, yes, America. Boom! Me, RPG, and boom!" The detainee's gestures grew more frantic.

"Wait, did he just say, 'RPG'?"

The interpreter asked him in Arabic and reported, "Yes, he says he shot an RPG at Americans, and then they blew up his house." This time, the interpreter was biting his lip to keep from laughing; I'm not sure if he was laughing at the idiot or us. Either way, both of us knew this guy's staple removal was about to get pretty painful.

The medic had been removing the first staples as gently as possible. It was still pretty painful, judging from his grimaces and his squirming. The medic kept telling him, "Sorry, but I'm going as easy as I can."

I told him not to worry, that the guy was hurt shooting RPGs at Americans. After that, the medic quickly removed the staples without all the previous niceties. That detainee started yelling though. All this happened before the medic even reached his upper thigh on the first leg; he still had the torso, both arms, and the other leg to finish. Needless to say, by the time the medic was finished, I had quite the headache, and detainee Rocket Man was nearly unconscious.

Admittedly, we handled different situations in Bucca quite callously, but violence was the norm there. It wasn't shocking, and we didn't even pay much attention when a detainee was jumped and beaten by others. Stabbings and rapes as punishment, especially in the Hastys, weren't unusual either. In fact, the days when violence didn't happen were rare. I used to tell my compound chiefs that I didn't care what they did to each other as long as they gagged the person they were beating or raping. I didn't want to hear the screams. By this point, my conscience wasn't bothered anymore. The incidents were simply annoying.

One particular evening, I was in the tower next to the gates. It was almost shift change, so I had thrown my bag down to the base of the tower. A few detainees brought a blanket baby up to the gate of Quad A. This guy was in really bad shape with blood coming from his head, nose, mouth, and all over his body. He had either been stabbed or beaten with sticks. Some of the guards came over to drag him out of the shark gate, leaving a nice trail of blood in the dirt, while another guy looked for the medic. As the guys dragged him out, they almost hit my backpack with him. I started yelling from the tower, "Hey watch my backpack! I don't want his fucking blood all over it. I don't know what diseases he has."

Once I was relieved from the tower, I climbed down and inspected my backpack for blood. Thankfully, none was on it. The detainee was still lying there, waiting for the medic, who was apparently on lunch break. I grabbed my backpack and headed to the trucks; I never even checked to see if he had lived. I didn't care. That was just the way life was there; gradually, you came to care only for your people. You became desensitized to the pain and suffering of everyone else. We learned to shut down feelings, such as compassion. They were unnecessary and useless.

"O'Brien! I know you can hear me! Stop shooting. The Captain is on his way out!" Taylor's voice kept cutting in and out over the radio in my tower. Mostly it was cutting out because I kept pressing the key down and cutting her off. She hated it when I did that. The detainees were acting a little stupid again, so we were shooting anyone who stuck their head out of the tents. Unfortunately, our Army leadership did not approve of this and kept telling us not to fire. By this point of the deployment, nobody really cared or respected any leadership other than our own immediate superiors, Army be damned. But Taylor was at least giving us a heads up that the captain was coming. And just like the time before, by the time he arrived, no one was firing or rioting.

I was starting to have a curious phobia as time wore on. Right before the November crew left, one of their sergeants started wearing face shields on his helmet all the time. One day, I asked him why, and he told me he was worried about getting hit in the eye and ending up at home with a black eye. At the time, I thought he was a little nutty and paranoid. Later, I wasn't so sure. I was completely convinced that a chai rock would hit me and break my nose. I knew that it would happen; I could feel it in my bones. We all knew that the end was coming but still didn't have any particular time frame, so I tried to keep a grip on my paranoia.

One day, I was standing with an airman on the back side of Quad A, watching the detainees throw some rocks at a few of the towers. A Humvee drove up behind us, so I turned to see who it was. As I did, a small rock caught the back left side of my helmet. Even though it was quite small, I almost lost my balance due to the force.

Later that night, once I took off my helmet, I had a pretty little knot growing.

Another time, I was in one of our towers, again watching Quad A, with A1C Burke. He was from my home base, and for a while, I was even his supervisor. He had asked me to climb up into the tower to watch a few detainees. He couldn't tell if they were trying to tunnel, but something was wrong with one of the HESCOs. I got up there, and sure enough, sand was pouring down the HESCO as if someone had opened a hole in the bottom and all the dirt on top were falling down. I called TSgt Hai over the radio and told him we needed to pull the detainees for a head count immediately. They were definitely digging a tunnel.

Once the detainees realized Burke and I were watching them, they began showering our tower with rocks and shit bags. Since our instructions were not to shoot unless we had a clear target, I told Burke to shoot at whoever started throwing stuff while I stuck my arm out the door. As I did, I immediately got pegged three times in the bicep. It would have hurt, but two things stopped it initially. 1) My arm seemed to go numb after the first rock. 2) I had apparently gone oddly deaf. I forgot that the firing of a shotgun in a small space is incredibly loud, and for a few seconds, neither of us could hear a thing.

Once I regained my hearing, the first thing I heard was a string of swear words, beautifully put together by Burke. I kept yelling, "What's wrong?"

I thought he had been hurt. He had been hit right in the side of the face with a shit bag. He was almost out of control with rage; I had to grab him to keep him from climbing out the window of the tower. Finally, I calmed him down enough to get him to go down and get scrubbed off. While he climbed down, I shot at any detainees I could see so, hopefully, he didn't get hit again. After everything quieted down and the detainees were in the holding area, we discovered a tunnel going toward the burn pit and one very dead detainee who had been suffocated by the dirt. Later that evening, as I got back to my hut, my arm started hurting. For a minute, I forgot what had happened, and then I saw the pretty little bruises. So I had a great reason for my paranoia.

As I walked around to the front of our Hasty guard shack, I suddenly stopped short. Right near the door stood an Air Force Lt. Col., a Chief, and a First Sergeant. Of course, I was the only NCO at the compound. TSgt Hai was at a meeting with our Army leadership in the TOC, and Sgt Gleason was off. *Fuck my life.* Inwardly cursing, I went over, snapped to attention, and introduced myself. The Lt. Col. looked at me quizzically, and finally the Chief said, "SSgt O'Brien, don't you salute officers?"

These guys were new or lost. "No, sir, no one salutes officers in the prison. Sometimes the detainees single out higher-ranking officers and try to hurt them." To emphasize the point, my radio started squawking about some of them flinging poop right then.

We exchanged some proper niceties, and the whole time, I couldn't figure out who they were. We hadn't seen any Air Force leadership since our commander left in August; since that time, we had been under Army leadership at the Hastys. After about five minutes, the First Sergeant stated, "Well, we are surprised to find any Air Force out here. We thought all our people were in the TIF."

Now I knew who they were; they had replaced our commander but never come to check on us. I tried to keep my growing anger in check. "Well, sir, all of *your* people are in the TIF. Out here are only the February crew. You know, the people you were supposed to replace."

After an awkward silence, the Lt. Col. had the audacity to say they didn't even realize any Air Force were working the Hastys and they had wandered over to us accidentally. Apparently, they got lost trying to find the TIF, and when they stopped at an Army Hasty to ask for directions, they mistakenly sent them down to us.

I asked if they would like a quick tour, knowing that I had to but also kind of hoping one of them would get hit with a shit bag. I started walking them around the area, first showing them the quad gates and front towers. The occasional rock and poop would fly over; after a few minutes, they said it was enough. The Colonel asked if the detainees rioted like this every day; I laughed out loud at that and told him this wasn't even close to a riot. It was simply their normal behavior. I said he really should have seen the riots in the TIF. This was just a minor tantrum.

Later that night, while I was telling Taylor, Gina, and Rachel about the visit, I got so mad. So did they. It was simply unbelievable that our commander had been gone almost two months, and not only had the new one not been over to see us, but he didn't even realize we were there. I had no idea who they were when they showed up at Hasty 31. I didn't know their names, nothing. Their whole leadership was hands off with us; from when Col. Shell left until we started parting ways in Kuwait, only a few Captains were in charge of us.

In order to save face and to make sure our crew knew that the new leadership was in charge, they scheduled a mortar response exercise a couple of weeks later. Exercises were only conducted at air bases, which Camp Bucca was not, and they weren't done under certain threat conditions, like a deployment where real mortars happened quite often. Since it was only for the Air Force personnel and we were in a high threat condition, they had to tell us the day and approximate time it would happen. Because we always got a heads up before real mortar attacks!

So on the day and time that we were supposed to be ready to respond to this mortar attack, Taylor and I decided to go take a shower while waiting for the sirens to go off. They started going off around the time we were done and getting dressed. We took our time, walking back to our hut to drop off our shower supplies, strolling over to the head count spot. You could tell which crew people were in by how they responded: the June crew was properly responding quickly and jogging; the February crew was lazily walking and talking while responding.

Needless to say, leadership was not impressed with our attitude or response time. The senior leadership started calling for us to fall into formation. Just to show how split our two teams were, we automatically fell into two different formations. Our captains had us form up separately from the June team. A senior NCO from their crew came over and started chewing us out about how terrible and lackadaisical our response time was. "What if that had been a real attack? How would you have responded then?" He kept yelling.

Finally, some unknown person yelled back, "We *have* had real attacks. Shut the fuck up." Nobody ever found out who said that, but that senior NCO was pissed.

If that exercise was supposed to help us mesh with the June crew, it didn't. If anything, it pulled us even further apart. A few of our crew stayed in the TIF the whole time and worked with them. I have no doubt that most of them were decent guys, but many of us were simply fed up with the Air Force by the time they showed up. It wasn't their fault, but we had become angry, bitter, and salty and disliked any new people by the time they arrived. I'm convinced Jesus himself could have been one of the new guys, and still, we would have been pissed.

After that, Air Force leadership left us alone. I never saw any of the leadership at the Hastys or anywhere else again. When we finally did leave Bucca, none of them came out to wish us farewell or see us off.

CHAPTER TWENTY

FILTH IN THE RANKS

The detainees weren't always the bad guys even though we liked to pretend they were. We did our own share of breaking the law too; however, the rules were different, depending on who you were, what the crime was, and such. For example, General Order #1, also known as the no-sex rule, stated all the areas where two people couldn't have sex but never actually said that they couldn't do the physical act. The exact punishment would depend on who those two people were. If a male and female were both enlisted, both officers, single, well-liked, etc., the punishment wouldn't be too bad. If the female got pregnant or if either of them were married, then the punishment was worse. But that was the military justice portion; there was also a whole side of public opinion.

With Bucca public opinion, it always came down to the detainee level. If your crime had nothing to do with Iraqis, detainees, or hurting fellow servicemen, it wasn't considered that bad. With that said, we also had a hierarchy of crimes that had nothing to do with the actual breaking of the law. The worst crime ever was to be considered a Delta Lima, which was the phonetic alphabet for

Detainee Lover. For example, I could sleep with a married man but still command more respect than a Sergeant who gave his detainees extra perks, such as a movie or soccer ball.

We began hearing whispers of a terrible crime, a rumor that an airman had committed an immortal sin. She had slept with a detainee. No one knew exactly who it was, but the rumor gained more traction every day. This was possibly the worst thing anyone could have done while at Bucca. First, why wouldn't this person just sleep with another service member or, if it had to be an Iraqi, an ICO? What the hell would ever possess someone to have sex with a detainee? This wasn't the beginning of our deployment; we knew exactly who they were: poop, semen, piss-flinging animals.

At first, I thought it was just a nasty rumor, but the more it gained popularity, the more it sounded possible. Then suddenly, a compound number was attached to the rumor. It was the same compound Gina worked at, so the next time I saw her at our hut, I asked her if it were true. "Heather, I can't talk about it because the investigation is still ongoing, but let's just say some awful shit occurred at the compound."

That's all she would say; I didn't push her because I didn't want her to feel pressured to talk about something still being investigated, and also, I was a little scared to know.

Later, we found out that it was true, but we were given the wrong person's name. It was not an airman but, in fact, a staff sergeant who committed this atrocity. Not only did SSgt Rancid Ass have sex with a detainee, but she did it in the most disgusting place: their toilet area. She also gave the detainee keys to the interior gates, and they took pornographic photos of each other. She used an airman's camera to take the photos, and when the investigation began, she tried to frame the airman.

For a while, it worked as far as the rest of us knowing who did what. For years, I thought that airman was the culprit. But she wasn't. Many of us thought this because she was flown out of Bucca right when the whole investigation started. She left because she was testifying at the trial. Her deployment lasted for over a year by the end, because she had to stay in Kuwait until the trial ended. Many of us saw her there and were terribly cruel to her. This continued until SSgt Rancid Ass appealed the tribunal's decision, which made the entire case file public knowledge.

This was by far the worst crime any of us could even imagine. To have had sex with a detainee was, in most people's eyes, about the same as bestiality. Personally, I would have more respect for someone who fucked a donkey. It was probably a good thing that nobody knew who the culprit was until after she had left the base because someone would have attacked her. To this day, I get disgusted when I think about what SSgt Rancid Ass did—not only the act of having sex with a detainee but then the audacity to blame it on an airman, someone she should have been training and mentoring. The whole situation was vile. I also feel terrible about the way we treated the other airman later when we saw her in Kuwait and how awful we talked about her. Monsters came in all shapes and sizes at Bucca, but to fuck a detainee was a level of monstrosity that even other monsters reviled.

CHAPTER TWENTY-ONE

"I'LL KILL YOU"

Working at 31 was always interesting. One day, I arrived at work to find that our second quad had been filled overnight. The detainees weren't new to the Hastys; they had just been moved from one of the Army quads because during head count, one detainee was reported missing. A search was conducted, and he wasn't found. Intel reported that he might be dead somewhere in the quad, so the whole group was moved over to our empty quad while a thorough dig and evacuation was done. After about a week, the detainee was found minus his head, arms, and legs. As far as I know, those were never found. These were the people we dealt with; they had no problem killing one of their own. What would they do to us if given the chance?

This new group was placed in Quad B, and they were total assholes. Often, they would refuse to listen to anything we said, especially if the guard was female or Black. I told TSgt Hai that Quad B really had an attitude issue, and he asked me what we should do about it. "We give them an all-female guard group for a while until they realize that they won't get anything until they work with females," I said. He agreed that was a good idea, so for the next week or so, only females interacted with Quad B. To say the detainees were beyond pissed is an understatement. I told their chief to get them ready for head count and dinner; he refused to look at or even answer me. I told him that until the quad lined up for head count, I couldn't give them their dinner. He still refused to speak to me, so no dinner. This went on for three days. Finally, he called the group to line up for head count.

Two female airmen conducted the head count while I stood on the shark cage with the shotgun. In the back of my mind, I was sure that today would be the day someone would shank my foot through the metal slats. I was high-stepping around as much as possible; the two airmen kept laughing at my weird jumps and leaps. As the detainees were making their way through the head count, a particularly rowdy group of about eight-to-ten men in the middle of the walkway started yelling and trying to disrupt the process. At first, I told them to shut up, or I would hit them with the shotgun. They ignored me, so I told their quad chief to shut them up, or I would discipline the whole group because of their unruliness. They ignored him too. One guy in particular seemed to egg them on but not actively create the ruckus; he let the others do it for him. Finally, I got so irritated, I pulled my loaded M9 out of the holster (a big no-no) and told him that if those men didn't shut up, I would shoot him. Not them, him. Instantly, they were silent; not a single person spoke for the rest of the head count. Because of their reaction, I had the airmen mark his inmate number as a possible person of importance. Once head count was over, I told the quad chief that because his people were so unruly during the lineup, they would have to wait until we finished our quad search before they got dinner. That evening, I earned a new nickname from the detainees, the Bitch or *Aleahira* in Arabic. It denotes a singular person, like the head, not one of many. My parents always said to strive to be the best at whatever you do.

I told TSgt Hai about the head count shenanigans and how we might have found a good intel source. He was less than enthused by my methods, both the food withholding and gun waving, but intrigued by who that detainee might be. I explained I hadn't been withholding food; they wouldn't line up, so I couldn't be sure if I had enough for everyone. As for the gun waving, I wasn't waving it; I very clearly pointed at a particular object and was ready to use it. At that point, he simply sighed and shook his head. "SSgt O'Brien, you aren't in QRF anymore. You have to learn how to work with these detainees in order to get them to do what needs to be done."

I replied, "TSgt Hai, I will never work with or compromise with them. They will do what I say or suffer the consequences. That's the only way I'll do things." Poor guy, I know he was only trying to teach me how to deal with them, but I don't think he fully realized my hatred for them.

"Hey, SSgt O'Brien, did you hear about the intel that MI [Military Intelligence] got from that detainee you spotted last week?" The airman speaking seemed pretty excited about this information. I had almost forgotten about the detainee causing a ruckus during head count. Apparently, MI had finally gotten a hold of him and interrogated him. As usual, MI wasn't telling us much about what he knew, only that it was a good catch and the information was of some importance.

A couple of days later, TSgt Hai told Sgt Gleason and I that the detainee would be getting moved to the SHU. There are limits for how long a detainee is to be placed in the SHU; either 90 or 120 days was the maximum at the time. When I asked TSgt Hai how long he would stay there, TSgt Hai said that he would remain in the SHU indefinitely per order of the TIF Commander. Whoa! Our TIF commander was a big detainee-loving asshole, so if he wanted the guy there for a long time, then the detainee must have really been important.

We were tasked with figuring out a way to get the detainee out of his quad without causing a riot and without too much resistance from him. MI told us that he was quite proficient in a few martial arts, plus we had often seen him teaching other detainees physical fitness, so he was in great shape. We decided to get him out with the easiest and oldest method; we told him he had a visitor in the front of the prison.

Sgt Gleason told the quad chief to bring him up so we could take him to the visitation area. Since he had an issue with me, I was up in the tower, watching the transport team while they handcuffed and shackled him. He came up to the gate quite easily, and once the cuffs were placed on him, he was brought out, and the transport team began to belly chain and shackle him. He realized something was off; he looked up at the tower as I waved at him, armed with my M4 set to fire, safety off. He had been caught and went quietly to the bus, mumbling under his breath but not really resisting. If he still had any doubts, they were lost when he got on the bus; it was totally empty save the driver and guards from the SHU.

We had been told our relief was finally on its way; they weren't Air Force but an Army Guard unit. "On their way" is quite the ambiguous term. For all we knew, they were in the States or Kuwait or not even formed up yet—that's how the military worked.

But after this particular detainee was moved, I didn't work in the Hastys much longer, at least not where I would be interacting with the detainees. TSgt Hai made me a rover, checking on the towers and a post way in the back of the compound. I didn't mind it; it was a break being away from the detainees, and I thought he was only being nice. He was, but he was also being careful. After the detainee left, his old quad placed a hit out on me. TSgt Hai was smart enough not to tell me until after we left the Hastys for the final time; he knew that if I knew about the threat, I would have demanded to work around them all the time. Not because I wanted to die but just to prove I didn't care about their threats although, truthfully, by that point, I didn't really care about living or dying. By then, I really believed that I would never leave Bucca alive. I accepted that the only way I would leave would be when I died.

CHAPTER TWENTY-TWO

RELIEF BUT NO FREEDOM

T hen, one day, it happened! I woke up early and left my hut, heading to the cadillac. On my way back, I was blindly trying to walk without opening both eyes because I forgot my sunglasses and the Iraqi sun at 0900 hours is blazing! I was also hoping to get maybe a few more minutes of rest before really starting the day. Someone called my name, and I couldn't figure out who it was because I was so blinded by the damn sun. I finally spotted a Master Sergeant from my crew yelling to me. I went over to him and asked what he needed. He said I was officially relieved from work; on top of that, I was going to be part of a crew headed to Kuwait to start getting our area set up for the rest of the crew to arrive. Then he walked away. Just like that, I was no longer going to work: no more detainees, no more prison. I wish I could say I was excited, but really, I felt utterly confused and a little lost.

I went back to the hut and told Taylor the news. I didn't quite believe it and thought I was dreaming or sleepwalking. It just didn't seem possible. A special team in Kuwait needed to set up accommodations for our crew. That didn't sound realistic and definitely not like something a mere Staff Sergeant would be doing. It sounded more like a job for a Master Sergeant. That evening, I went to the area where I had been told to rally up. About forty of us were there; we had a quick briefing, and then were released. I still had no idea what we were supposed to be doing in Kuwait, but it didn't matter because we had been told we weren't leaving for at least a couple of more days. Each day at our daily guard mount, more people were present, relieved of prison duty. On the second day, Taylor was relieved, and on the third day, Gina was. Rachel had already left for home a couple of weeks earlier; her husband was military too, and he was also deploying, which left no one to care for their child. For once, the Air Force took care of its people and sent her home.

So now everyone in our hut was officially off prison duty and man, were we bored. Probably the only thing worse than deploying and working in Bucca was deploying and not working while in Bucca. Each day at our guard mount, we had a very simple task to do for the whole day. One day, it was to turn in our ammunition: We had to go to the armory, block and count every single round, and then put it back in the magazines before turning them in. It was tedious but simple; after that, we had nothing left to do for the day. The next day, we had to put all our extra bags in the storage containers; we were officially living out of backpacks again. Not that it mattered too much as most of us had been washing our own laundry for months; the laundry service was terribly overworked, and many times, clothes came back dirty or still wet. I once had mold on my DCUs; after my underwear went missing, that was the last straw. I washed my own stuff from then on.

After three or four days of just hanging around the LSA, we were all beginning to go a little stir crazy. No one was used to sleeping more than four hours at a time, so our sleep schedules were really messed up with no work to prepare for. Finally, one day, we were told at guard mount that it was the big day; we would be leaving that night. Everyone was so excited; people were hugging and laughing for the first time in months. The rest of the day, everyone got their stuff ready, bought last-minute souvenirs from the haji shops, and waited for our call to leave. We waited and waited. For two days. Then three days. Then more. Apparently, dust storms on the border made it impossible to fly a helo to us. Funny that we were only five-to-seven miles from the border and our skies were clear with no wind or clouds. We had heard the "dust storm" excuse before; it was what leadership told us every time an Air Force headquarters team was supposed to visit and never showed up.

Finally, we were told to show up at the helo pad after dark. Taylor, Gina, and I finished cleaning our hut, making sure we didn't leave anything behind. We headed to the chow hall for one last light meal; helo rides tended to be pretty bumpy. Afterward, we went back to the hut, grabbed our backpacks, went over to billeting, and turned in our keys. Then we headed down to the helo pad where we waited for hours: all night long and into the early morning. Off in the distance came the faint *whop*, *whop* of helicopter blades. The first one landed, and the first group of people loaded up; they took off to our cheers and yells on the ground and I'm sure from those inside the helo as well.

About twenty to thirty minutes later, the next helo landed. It was my group's turn. Right as we lined up, Taylor turned around in front of me and did her best version of Mel Gibson's *Braveheart* by screaming at the top of her lungs, "*Freeeee-dom!*" What a terrible omen. Seconds later, the helo just took off with none of us inside. All the other flights out were canceled for the day too. We had just watched our ride land and then leave us again. It was beyond crushing.

I entered a state of borderline insanity. I began walking the mile back to the LSA so fast that neither Taylor nor Gina could keep up. I was mumbling to myself, probably at full volume; all I know is that absolutely no one would walk near me.

I walked right back into the billeting office and told them our helo left us, so I demanded our old hut back. The billeting sergeant told me that he had already given our hut to another group but we could go stay in the transient tents. I lost it. "You give me the keys to my hut, or I'll blow you all away!" I screamed while waving my M4 and M16/203 rifles around, one in each hand. Since I had absolutely no ammunition, he was less than impressed.

"Sergeant, you'd better calm down and think about what you're saying."

Luckily for me, Taylor walked in right then and pulled me back outside. "Are you crazy? You can't tell people you're going to kill them!"

I was still so mad, I shrugged her off and started walking away. My M16/203 strap had been chaffing my shoulder all night, and I finally took the thing off and threw it on the ground. "Stupid fucking weapon! Why do I have to carry three fucking weapons?" Still muttering, I left it on the ground and walked toward the transient tents. I think Taylor picked up the M16, but it might have been Gina.

At the transient tents, we entered our little area. It was awful. The room had three bunk beds and two lockers that didn't lock. On one bed was a large rock, just sitting there for no reason. A funny smell wafted through the air; we quickly realized that an old Uncrustables peanut-butter-and-jelly sandwich, the kind that is supposed to be frozen, was lying on a top bunk. It was baking in the 100-degree heat and at least a few days old. It was still in its wrapper, which did little to stop the smell of rotten jelly goo. Gina picked up the sandwich, I held the rock, and Taylor was still unsuccessfully trying to lock the locker full of weapons. We all looked at each other for a moment; I don't know who broke down first, but suddenly, we were sobbing with laughter. We weren't sure if we were laughing or crying; we didn't ever quite figure it out. Gina asked, "What do we do with these?" In true Bucca fashion, we found another empty room and put the rock and sandwich goo on beds in there. Fuck whoever found them later, poor bastards.

The next day, we were all sitting in the tent, trying not to remember where we were. I was attempting to sleep, using my poncho liner as a sheet and a DCU top as a pillow. Gina was listening to her iPod while reading, and Taylor was sleeping, or at least, I thought she was. A rowdy group right outside our tent was yelling, laughing, and playing some music. And of course, since it was a tent, we could hear everything. It became too much for Taylor; suddenly, she sat up and screamed, "*Shut uuuuupppp!*" Gina very calmly unplugged her earphone and looked at Taylor; I almost fell off the bed from a combination of shock and the fact that the beds were so small, sized for two-year-olds. Outside, there was utter silence; either everyone left, or they all had heart attacks. Taylor had now snapped; she looked at the tent side like it might talk back for a few seconds. Then she said, "That's what I thought," and rolled over and went back to sleep. The world of insanity had just claimed another victim.

CHAPTER TWENTY-THREE

WELCOME BACK TO THE AIR FORCE

A few days after our failed escape attempt, we were back at the helo pad for attempt number 2. This time, we were leaving in the middle of the day without the cover of night; no pilot wanted to fly during the day because of the danger of being shot down. I really didn't care—by this point, I didn't believe we would actually ever get on a helo. The first one arrived, and one group left. Five or ten minutes later, the second one arrived; another group, gone. I can't remember what group I was in or even boarding the helo, for that matter. I was on the helo, and it took off; I didn't want to listen to my iPod because I wanted to be able to hear the RPG or bullets that were going to shoot us down. I looked out the window as we flew over the TIF, one last look; I half believed we would crash right into one of the compounds. Then suddenly, we were over the berm of the base; I thought, *It's okay if we go down now. At least I made it out of Bucca. I can die happy.* Still, we kept flying—no RPGs or bullets. Hell, the pilot didn't even need to do any evasive maneuvers.

All of it was a blur: how long we were in the air and even where and when we landed. I had to ask another friend who was there for all this information. My brain refused to grasp that we had done it—we had left Bucca alive. We landed in an airfield on Camp Buehring. Our final destination was Ali Al Saleem Air Base, Kuwait, but we had to wait until all of us were out of Bucca. Even that day, not everyone got to leave; the last few group members, TSgt Holmes included, had to stay three more days until they could make it out.

There was a small covered area with picnic tables and some MREs to eat. Most of us wandered around quiet and in shock; no one was whooping or shouting. Little snippets of conversations floated around me. "Never thought I'd leave." "Can you believe we made it?" "It even smells cleaner here."

These words helped me realize I wasn't alone in my shock. Just like when I had been told I was done in the TIF, I almost felt let down, as if I had been ready to die, and now I was being forced to live. I wouldn't understand these reactions for years though. At that moment, I simply called it confusion and disbelief; maybe it was a very vivid dream, and I would soon wake up back in Bucca. By the expressions of many others, I wasn't the only one pondering that possibility.

We climbed onto several buses and headed to Ali Al Saleem, or just Saleem, as most people called it. The drive was pretty quiet and uneventful; I spent most of the ride looking out the window and listening to my iPod. I wondered how much of the road we had already been on when we were headed to Iraq. I chuckled. It was probably the exact same road, but I was totally different.

As we rolled up to the front gate, I was slightly shocked that we were truly entering an actual Air Force base. It may not seem like such a big deal to some, but many things are done differently on an Air Force base than an Army base, and well, we had forgotten most of that. We would soon find out just how much. At the front gate, an SF airman got on the bus to check our IDs; we were tired and definitely hungry, so we didn't give him a very hard time. He held his nose when he initially stepped on the bus, which was quite a common reaction over the next few days. Every person around us would have to take a few steps back at first.

As we drove around the base, I felt like a child coming home. There were planes: F-15s, C-130s, C-5s, all my old friends. The engines were rolling in a constant rhythm like a mother's bedtime singing; I had forgotten how normal those sounds were. When I heard them again, I realized we had truly left Bucca. For the next few days, I was caught up watching the planes take off and land; even though I'm not an enthusiastic flyer, seeing an actual airfield was a tangible reminder that we were back in the Air Force.

The buses dropped us off at the base armory where our weapons cases had been placed after they were pulled from the trailers. Each person had turned in all their ammunition at Bucca; however, we were given one magazine each for our helicopter ride. I'm not sure what one magazine would have accomplished in an extended firefight, but we never had to find out. We simply had to turn in the ammo, clear our weapons, and place them in our weapons cases. Here is where the differences between the Air Force and the Army became quickly apparent: The Air Force has nice little clearing barrels where a person properly clears their weapon; the Army has no such childish practice. Just don't point the weapon at other people while clearing it. So in true Army fashion, we all began clearing our weapons right where we were standing. I'm pretty sure the poor armorer's hair immediately turned gray. But in the end, they got all the live ammunition, and nobody got shot.

At this point, our Little Rock squad realized we had a problem: Somewhere between Iraq and Kuwait, an empty weapons case had gone missing. This made packing quite difficult because we now only had three cases instead of four, and we had to make all the weapons that were supposed to go in the fourth case fit in the other three. So we got to work, taking weapons apart and finding ways to stuff pieces into the other cases until everything fit. The only issue was that one case was above the allowed weight for aircraft. The sergeant in charge of getting our stuff loaded for overseas flights said not to worry about it; he would make sure they got on the plane.

Our next stop was a quick briefing about the air base and some crap that I didn't pay attention to. All I could think about was the chow hall next door and the fact that there was a tent filled with washers and dryers for laundry. Finally, the sergeant shut up and told us where the empty tents were; we were to decide how we filled them up. Then, we were released until the next day. We set up rooms in the tents in the usual way: first come, first served. Again, I was rooming with Taylor, A1C Torrey, and some stupid second Lt. who showed up at the last minute. Our room was really only a small cubicle with two bunk beds, one of three cubicles in the tent. Taylor, Torrey, and I dropped off our backpacks, quickly grabbed the beds we wanted, made them, and then headed out to grab some chow.

We made it about fifty feet from our tent before we began freaking out about where our weapons were. We had carried at least one—many times both—every day, everywhere for the past ten months. Not having them now was terrifying. Even though we were in Kuwait where it was safe, it still looked like southern Iraq: dusty desert just like Bucca. Plus, it was the Middle East; no place was truly safe. For the next few days, especially when I first got up in the morning, I suffered frightening anxiety attacks, trying to remember where I left my weapon.

When we entered the chow hall, everyone seemed to look at us as they stared and talked. As we walked past groups to get to the food line, their expressions spoke loud and clear. The head shake, cough, and scooting back told me that the prison smell had followed us and was aggressively offending their delicate senses. I was really starting to get angry. I had showered whenever I had the opportunity, and these were the cleanest DCUs I had. It's hard to clean a smell your nose doesn't notice anymore. I immediately began to think, *These stupid-ass Air Force people. They think they're better than us! They couldn't hack shit if they needed to.* I never even noticed that I immediately separated myself from my own branch. I instinctively began to think with an "us vs. them" mentality—I would do this for a long time.

After getting our trays, Taylor and I sat down. As I got ready to start eating, something about the tray seemed off. I stopped and began looking at my tray; Taylor asked what the problem was. "I don't know. The tray and stuff just look weird."

"O'Brien, it's because the plates are real, and the utensils are actual metal." Whoa! We had been eating with plastic utensils from Styrofoam trays for so long that regular items confused me. For a brief minute, I wondered if my brain had gotten so used to being animalistic that I had forgotten how to be normal; the coming days proved these fears to be true. We were all animals.

After eating, Taylor and I grabbed our clothes and headed over to the laundry tent. Torrey decided to go to the pool and do her laundry later. I was so excited about having a real washer and dryer to use again. I had been doing most of my own laundry for months. Our uniforms were all a different color than the Air Force guys at Saleem. All our clothes had a yellowish-brown tinge that made us stick out. We dropped off our clothes in the washers and headed back to the tents to relax. A little while later, we went back to put them in the dryers. Once the loads were finished, they were a different color. We were astounded! We had successfully washed Bucca out. But we really hadn't. Even though the brownish tinge had lessened, it was still there. Our clothes never matched the other Air Force members in Kuwait. We always stuck out.

Later that day, Torrey came back to the tent, laughing and telling us that our group was officially kicked out of the pool. Apparently, some of us got a little rowdy. When some officers asked us to quiet down, the group told them to fuck off. The real issue was there were officers from our group at the pool, and they did nothing to stop the altercation. In fact, they were laughing too. Later that night, a whole group of our crew snuck into the pool area after hours and started having a little party until the cops showed up and chased them off. Now we were all cops as well, and some of us knew the cops stationed at Saleem. None of them wanted to get us in trouble, but we weren't making it very easy for them.

The next day, we all had to report to the tent where we had our initial briefing; we had to do a very quick in-processing even though we would be leaving in a few days. While we were waiting for the briefing, about forty of us were standing around smoking. One of the sergeants, who was going to brief us, came up to us and said we were only supposed to smoke in the smoking area. Oops! Army bases don't have anything like that; we just had to smoke at least ten feet from a tent. Just another reminder that we were back with the Air Force.

Once we all got into the tent and settled down, the briefing began with the pool incidents. Base leadership had decided our group would be allowed to use the pool again if we promised to behave. Most of us just laughed at that; we were going to use the pool even if they said we couldn't. The briefings continued with information about the base and where to go if we were mortared or attacked. I stopped listening after that but tuned back in when the briefer talked about how it was the middle of Ramadan, and some locals worked on base. Apparently, they liked to use the smoke-pit gazebos during their prayer time. He added that if we saw them in the gazebo to please not smoke there because it would offend them. Most of us started laughing. A few people, including me, yelled that we didn't give a shit if they were offended. I leaned over to TSgt Hai, an avid smoker, and said, "What group does he think he is talking to? We don't care if we offend some fucking hajis. In fact, that makes our day better!"

TSgt Hai just chuckled. Finally, one of our captains told us all to quiet down, or we would have a mandatory formation afterward. We shut up quickly.

A little while later, we began the in-processing. We were called up and made our way from stations set up around the back of the tent. The briefer stated that most of us would be called by our base; however, a few would be called out of order. As he began calling names, I leaned over to TSgt Hai. "I guess he is calling the crazies first. Look, they have to go to Mental Health as their first stop." I laughed a little.

Then the briefer said, "SSgt O'Brien, please make your way to station one." My name was number four on a list of more than 250 people.

TSgt Hai looked at me and laughed. "Yep, the crazies for sure!"

I headed over to station one, Mental Health, and sat down with the officer at the booth. Curiosity was killing me. "Sir, why did I get called so early?"

"Well, sergeant, some of your paperwork here says you were in a lot of riots and violent incidents." It was true but no more than anybody else that worked in the prison. All of us dealt with riots and violent "incidents." I knew I was being lied to.

"Sir, everyone did that stuff. That's no explanation."

"Did you see people die?"

"I saw some detainees die, if that's what you mean."

"So you did see people die then?"

"Like I said, only detainees, not real people like any of us."

"Aren't detainees real people?"

"No, they're only detainees, not people."

As soon as the words left my mouth, I realized that I had just made a mistake. Not that I didn't believe my words, but the mental health technician would take it the wrong way. And he did. I was officially tagged as required to visit mental health during my in-processing when I returned to my home base. But to this day, I still wonder why I was singled out; I can only imagine it was because of my meltdown in May.

One nice advantage of being the fourth person was I finished much earlier than my squad. While I waited for them, I went out for a smoke, this time, in the designated smoking area. Once they were finished, we had a quick meeting and were released for the day until our mandatory formation after dinner. Taylor and I decided to check out the MWR (Military Welfare and Recreation) building; it supposedly had a small movie theater among other entertainment.

Once there, we walked around, checking it out. There was a little darkened room that served as the theater, an open area with some pool and ping-pong tables, and a little faux bar area that served sodas, tea, and my personal favorite, Monsters. I went to order, and imagine my shock when the airman taking orders behind the bar was none other than Amn B, the one we thought fucked detainees! She grabbed a Monster from the fridge, placed it on the countertop, and told me how much it was. Slowly recovering from my shock, I told her that I wouldn't take anything that had touched her hands. I don't really remember too much after that, just that I attempted to climb over the counter to attack her. But Taylor and another friend managed to grab me. For almost a year, the only way I had responded to any real or perceived threat were with quick and violent reactions. That was the only way I knew how to deal with stressors.

I wasn't the only one struggling with this. Someone accidentally called Taylor "Amn B" once. Now this person was stationed in Kuwait and had no idea what the rumor was, so it was truly an innocent mistake. But Taylor flipped out, told that person that she wasn't a detainee-fucking whore, and if the woman ever called her that name again, she would kick her ass. Now it was my turn to be the one holding someone back from attacking. Another person lost it on a Kuwaiti national who was working on the base. She saw him in an area that she didn't think he should be in, so she jumped him and almost choked him before someone pulled her off. It was common for any of us to start cursing out any Kuwaitis or third-country nationals (TCNs) that we ran into. Even though we were happy to be going home, the slightest provocation would set us off; anger was our normal reaction to anything out of our control or to any new situation.

CHAPTER TWENTY-FOUR

HAPPILY EVER AFTER?

E very evening after dinner, we assembled for mandatory formation. The officer in charge went over a few points: which groups were leaving the next day, any particular news we needed to know, where the Mental Health clinic was and the walk-in hours (this was re-emphasized every day), and if we had gotten in any more trouble that day. Each night, the formation was a little bit smaller; it felt as if our family were being split up rather than the end of a deployment. Gina's team was one of the first groups to go. One day, she was there, relaxing, and the next, gone as if she had never even been there. Finally, when we were culled down to about two hundred or so, we were told that all of us would be leaving the next day.

Moving that many people and that much gear takes some serious strategizing. Add to the fact that we were dealing with international travel with customs checks and weapons, and you have the perfect storm for a nightmare. We stayed in the staging area for five or six hours before going through a military customs inspection run by Navy personnel. It was very intense. Each person had to unpack every single bag and put all the items out on display for them to search. We each had at least three bags: a personal bag, an equipment bag, and an NBC (nuclear, biological, and chemical) gear bag. Each one had to be emptied one at a time to ensure items weren't placed in the wrong bag. Imagine the expression if the base supply guy went into an NBC bag and pulled out underwear. I thought about doing that just for fun.

After the customs check, we waited a few more hours. Each minute felt like years; we had almost nothing to do and no way to get comfortable. The chairs were simple hard plastic on a concrete floor that made any movement sound as if a desk were being scraped across tile. Plus, my mind was in this weird state of excitement and dread. I was excited to be going back home to my family, house, car, and all the creature comforts that I had missed. I was dreading this ending because this would probably be the last time I saw many of the people I had just lived with for ten months. These guys knew me better than my own family; we had shared experiences that I could never explain to others, and now, suddenly, we would be separated. Sure, some of them were going back to the same base, but the comradery wouldn't be the same. Even Taylor would be leaving; her time in the service was almost up. As soon as we got back to Little Rock, she was out-processing the Air Force.

Eventually, we were taken to the buses that would carry us to Kuwait City International Airport. Once we all were seated, this airman came by and told us that we were not supposed to listen to any radios, pull up the window shades, or sleep. We began to openly laugh at him; probably the nicest thing we said to him was "shut the fuck up." Most other comments involved him and a camel. After about twenty minutes of waiting, we headed to the airport. I listened to my iPod and looked out the window while Taylor napped next to me. I took those last few minutes to try to understand why I felt like I was leaving too early, like I would actually miss the shithole prison and Iraq. The dark Kuwaiti desert gave me no answers and even less comfort.

At KCIA, we bypassed entering the airport; the buses took us directly to the tarmac. We filed out and walked straight to the plane. There, Taylor and I finally disagreed heatedly—of all things, over where to sit. Both of us are very stubborn, so for the whole flight back to the States, we sat in different areas and wouldn't talk. At our layover in Germany, a mutual friend forced us to take a picture. In the photo, Taylor is on one side of our friend, and I'm on the other. We had scooted far away from each other and were not smiling. We laugh when we talk about it today; of all the craziness we went through, and that is what we got so pissed about. It was stupid, and I regret that I didn't get one last flight, hanging out with my friend.

The closer we got to America, the less excited I began to feel. All I could think about was getting back to my house that night and getting delightfully drunk. I *was* excited about that. Many of my friends had family meeting them at the airport, but my family was out of town in Egypt, of all places. I left the Middle East, and they went to it! Not that it was a big deal; I really wanted to get back to my house and be left alone for a while. Frankly, after all my nightmares, I was a little scared to be around my family. The end of my deployment was like waking up from a nightmare and yet wanting to be back in it. When we landed, I focused on getting through customs and check-in as quickly as possible so I could have my first beer before getting on our connecting flight.

After we landed and got off the plane, customs was a breeze, which seemed extremely odd since we were bringing back weapons and gear. None of the officials really wanted to look through our stuff. They just waved us on with a quick smile and "welcome home." I grabbed my bags and assigned weapons case and headed toward check-in with my squad. Taylor and I were cautiously talking again; both of us apologized for being assholes, and then we laughed at the stupidity of our fight. We got in line at the check-in counter, mumbling about how stupid it was that we were on different flights.

Because of all our gear, we couldn't fly on one plane; we would exceed the weight limit.

When I got to the counter, I placed each bag on the scale to check the weight. Last up was my assigned weapons case: the overloaded case that was ten pounds over the airline's weight limit. The conversation that followed showed how little patience I now had.

Airline clerk: Ma'am, your case is over the weight limit. I will need you to please lighten the load.

Me: Umm, this is a weapons case. It has only weapons inside it. I can't lighten it because I can't take anything out.

Clerk: Well, it will need to be lightened somehow. Do you need to take everything in this box?

Me, now irritated: Well, one of the grenade launchers is about ten pounds. What if I take one of those out? Can I bring it on the plane as a second carry-on, or would you prefer that I leave it over there in the trash can?

Clerk, looking angry and terrified: Why would you need so many guns?

(I'm losing it now. I'm in full military clothing along with about thirty other people in line. What in the hell does she think is going on?) Me, dead-pan serious: Because ma'am, when the revolution begins, we are going to need all these weapons. What the fuck do you think I need them for? Where is your manager?

After a couple of minutes, the manager made his way over to the counter and easily overrode the weight limit, telling the lady it was okay to make exceptions for government cases. As I was laughing at her, she marked my ticket, smiled, and sarcastically said, "Welcome home."

I looked at her, laughed again, and said, "Yeah, fuck you too."

Once in line at security, I was almost drooling for the beer I knew was on the other side. I just had to buzz through the checkpoint, and I was home free. Right as I was ready to go through the metal detector, the TSA agent looked at my ticket and said, "Ma'am, could you please step over here? You have been selected for a random search."

Now I was pissed! I tried to keep it in check because the TSA guys had a job to do and did have random selections. But I had to know, so as I was taking my DCU top off, I asked the TSA lady if my search was really random or if I had a marker from the airline check-in clerk. She kind of chuckled and said that some clerks tag tickets and some searches are random.

I just laughed. "I know it's the lady from the counter. That *bitch* is just trying to get back at me for being right at the check-in."

At that point, the TSA agent simply said, "Oh forget, doing this. Here is your ticket. Your search is clean. Have a good day." I smiled and walked off.

Rude as it was, this was how we lived every day during the whole deployment. Profanity, anger, and violence were the norm. If a person challenged you, the only reaction was to escalate until someone backed down; I attempted to make sure that was not me whenever I could help it. Depending on the person—a higher-ranking NCO or officer, my supervisor, or someone I respected—I would easily back down, but anyone else was fair game. If you backed down, especially in the TIF and with the detainees, then they would own you, and even your own crew wouldn't respect you. Once I returned home, everyone seemed too conditioned to being quiet and wimpy, or at least, that's how they seemed to me. I no longer understood how to act in a so-called civilized society, and a part of me didn't really care to learn.

After getting through security, I was finally home free to get that drink. I stopped at the first bar where a bunch of my team were already in line. We were whooping it up then: yelling, passing beers down the line, and all in all, having a great time. I then truly began to believe I would make it back home. I did not yet understand just how messed up my head was, but I finally realized that home was a reality, not a distant dream.

After quickly gulping two beers down, we made it right on time for our flight. On the flight, the airline attendants passed out two free beers as a welcome-home gesture. On our connecting flight in Dallas, the attendants gave us another free beer. That made five beers in about six hours, which most regular drinkers could handle. But we weren't regular drinkers anymore; ten months of dry living made us all lightweights. On the last flight, I kept cracking up at the other sergeant with me for no reason whatsoever as we discussed the cloud formations. None of this would have been too bad if our commanding officer, Major Fields, hadn't come to the airport to greet us. I made a great first impression on him as I strolled drunkenly right up to him and slurred out the words, "Hey, you're the new guy!" After making a complete ass of myself, he never liked me.

We were driven from the airport to our squadron where most of us picked up our car or house keys and headed home. I said hi to some friends working, grabbed my car keys, and headed to the Class Six store to buy a shitload of alcohol. We were all still pretty drunk from our flights, but no one had a problem with us driving around base.

Once I was back at my house, the first thing I did was open a beer and take the longest shower ever. The person taking care of my house had been deployed while we were still gone, so my house wasn't in great condition. Half the lights didn't work, and the A/C wasn't turning on, but I didn't care. I was determined to get drunk as a skunk and just enjoy the night alone. I kept going outside most of the night; I couldn't get over how green and lush it was. But even at home, something felt off. I kept waiting for Bucca to come back, waiting for rockets, riots, or violence from somewhere. I felt very alone.

Leaving Bucca hadn't cured the anger and hatred that was

seething through my body. If anything, it had only made it worse. Before, I was angry at detainees; now, I was angry at almost everything and everyone. I was mad that the world had continued to move on while we were gone. I was confused that nobody seemed to understand the barbaric conditions at Camp Bucca. I was scared that I couldn't seem to move on and get used to being back in the States. I was afraid that I would never trust anyone again. I couldn't understand how I was so glad to be out of Iraq and yet I missed it so badly I could almost cry. All these conflicting emotions overwhelmed me, so I reacted the only way I knew how: in anger. I began to alienate myself from the people I cared most about because I was scared that I would do something to hurt them. I told myself that pushing them away was the healthiest thing for them and me. I drank excessively every day for years. It was the only way that I could feel normal emotions; at least, that's what I told myself.

I tried mental health counseling and went during my in-processing, but I left their office angrier than ever. The female counselor kept trying to compare my experiences to that of Vietnam veterans. I kept telling her that those were not comparable experiences. Vietnam was some real combat shit; I simply guarded a prison. She threw out words like PTSD and adjustment disorder; I bristled at that. I didn't think that prison duty qualified me for those diagnoses. Plus, PTSD was a death knell to a Security Forces career at the time; if a commander heard that, they had to pull a person's weapons clearance. And no clearance meant you couldn't perform your job duties. Now you weren't a returning defender; now you were just broken, a weight on the squadron. Most people who got their clearance pulled for PTSD didn't get it back. So I fought tooth and nail to make sure no one labeled me with that. Plus, I didn't believe I had it and still really don't a lot of the time. I know people who have PTSD, who have gone through some terrible, horrific situations—things that would crush me—they are stronger than I could ever be.

But something was different about me; many people said so. Somewhere, my head had broken a little. I was constantly angry to the point of often physically shaking for no reason. At work as a police officer, I didn't always wait for backup, especially during domestic violence incidents. I wasn't suicidal; I just didn't care anymore. The intense thrill of unknown life-and-death situations that Camp Bucca provided on a daily basis was gone. I missed not knowing what crazy or violent events might happen at work; even my job as a cop wasn't exciting enough anymore. My brain buzzed all the time and never shut down. The only way to quiet it was drinking, every day and whenever possible. Soon, I had to drink in order to sleep after work but never before work. I refused to do that—in my head, as long as I didn't drink before work, then I didn't have a problem.

After a while, even that wasn't enough. My mind was still in a constant state of overload. It wouldn't be until seven years later— after one accidental suicide attempt, one intentional suicide attempt, and one psych ward vacation—before I was finally diagnosed as bipolar. My deployment didn't completely cause the condition, but the craziness of that place certainly helped push me further along the road into it.

The bitterness I held against the Air Force for abandoning us to the Army only grew. I disliked any leadership, especially my immediate chain of command. Some of them were okay, but I never went so far as to actually trust them. I had learned the bitter truth that the military will do what it needs to sustain operations. The term "fuck your feelings" definitely defines operation tempos and deployment schedules.

I wouldn't have been nearly as mad if our deployed leaders and wing commanders would have just said, "You're going to be here until you leave." No fake leave dates and no extensions, those only served to further erode any bit of morale and trust. I wouldn't have enjoyed the extensions, but I could have respected and understood that more than the continued bullshit: the moving of goals and promises of one more month, two more months, and on and on. I also never forgot the lieutenant colonel who didn't even know who we were in the Hastys; to this day, that awful example of leadership leaves a bitter taste in my mouth.

Time moved on. I finally got out of the Air Force in 2009, but I was still restless. Odd things triggered my anger and anxiety. Detainees wore yellow jumpsuits, so the sight of that color automatically set me on guard, and I was immediately ready for a violent confrontation with that person. Movies with violence or explosions wouldn't bother me too much, but if they had loud Arabic prayers in the background, I was immediately back in the TIF, surrounded by thousands of detainees praying and rioting. I would cover my ears or turn off the movie. Time and distance have slowly worn down these reactions.

I finally got help for my drinking and mental health problems. In group therapy, I was surrounded by other people who understood what it's like to be mentally broken. We may have all taken different paths, but our destination was the same, and in time, healing began.

Today, I look back on my deployment, and my only regret is letting the monster out. Despite the difficulties, I wouldn't trade the people I met along the way for anything. Those of us who have been there, regardless of when, have seen humanity at its worst. On both sides of the wire, people turned into monsters. But the majority refused to let the monster continue to rule; they fought their way back to their family and friends. Some of us took longer than others to come back. But no matter how long we took, most of us made it.

EPILOGUE

Not a day goes by that I don't think about my deployment. I can still hear the riots and fires if I listen hard enough. Some days, Iraq is very close. Every May and on June 9, I remember Micah, SSgt Sand, and the hottest rocket attack ever. At night, I sometimes see detainees fighting, escaping, rioting. But they no longer cause anger and hate and are now just a nostalgic memory and longing for battles past.

It wasn't until 2018 that I finally began to find peace. My restless soul hit the end of the road, and if something didn't dramatically change, I would end up in the hospital again or worse, successful in another suicide attempt. The monster within me would finally win once and for all. I could easily shrug off the idea for a while until I began seeing suicide notifications, first from friends of friends and then from some of my own friends. I wasn't the only one fighting monsters. Even though my life was going well, death was whispering my name once more.

Then, the God of my youth stepped back into my life. This wasn't a stained-glass Jesus, too apathetic and sickly to deal with my mess.

This was the Savior who walked right into my chaos and loved me through every dark night and painful memory. He is the real Jesus, who has been restoring my life ever since I said yes to His calling.

"You've gone into my future to prepare the way, and in kindness you follow behind me to spare me from the harm of my past .... You have laid your hand on me! It's impossible to disappear from you or to ask the darkness to hide me, for your presence is everywhere, bringing light into my night" (Psalm 139:5, 11).

He keeps this promise to me every day. Through every awful memory, through every dark whisper, and when the monster begins to growl again, He reminds me that He was there even when I didn't know it. And He is the One who silenced the monster forever.

ACRONYMS

A1C – Airman First Class

AF – Air Force

AFB – Air Force Base

C-wire – concertina wire (coils of razor wire)

Capt. – Captain

Col. – Colonel

DCU – Desert Camouflage Uniform

FN 303 – compressed air projectile launcher

ICO – Iraqi Correction Officer

IED – Improvised Explosive Device

ISIS – Islamic State of Iraq and Syria

K-9 – canine (dog)

KCIA – Kuwait City International Airport

LSA – Living Support Area

Lt. – Lieutenant

Lt. Col. – Lieutenant Colonel

M4 – carbine (shortened version of the M16A2 Assault Rifle)

M9 – Beretta semi-automatic handgun

M16 – Assault Rifle

MP – Military Police

MRE – Meals Ready to Eat

MSgt – Master Sergeant

NCO – Non-commissioned Officer

OC – Oleoresin Capsicum (pepper spray)

OEF – Operation Enduring Freedom (Afghanistan)

OIF – Operation Iraqi Freedom

QRF – Quick Response Force

REV 113 – Revised M113 Armored Personnel Carrier

Sgt – Sergeant

SSgt – Staff Sergeant

TIF – Theater Internment Facility

TSgt – Technical Sergeant

RPG – Rocket-propelled Grenade

SF – Security Forces

SHU – Special Handling Unit

SNCO – Senior Non-commissioned Officer

SrA – Senior Airman

WC – Wash Closet

ABOUT THE AUTHOR

Raised in a small town in Missouri, Heather O'Brien was an Army brat and a pastor's kid. She served in the military from May 2002 to March 2009. She was deployed to Bucca, Iraq, the location of this book, from mid-January 2007 to October 2007.

She now lives in Kansas City with her dog Albus, a Labradoodle. In her spare time, she enjoys doing mud runs and, as of the date of publication, will have completed at least six. She's been told she should do stand-up comedy although she's never tried it. At least not yet.

Contact Heather at: heatherobrien84@hotmail.com

Made in the USA
Las Vegas, NV
04 November 2022

58752557R00114